S0-AXL-411

THE WORLD'S GREATEST COMIC MAGAZINE

WRITER: JONATHAN HICKMAN
ARTIST: DALE EAGLESHAM

COLOR ARTIST: PAUL MOUNTS
LETTERER: VIRTUAL CALLIGRAPHY'S RUS WOOTON
COVER ARTISTS: ALAN DAVIS, MARK FARMER & JAVIER RODRIGUEZ
ASSOCIATE EDITOR: LAUREN SANKOVITCH
EDITOR: TOM BREVOORT

COLLECTION EDITOR: **JENNIFER GRÜNWALD**
ASSISTANT EDITOR: **ALEX STARBUCK**
ASSOCIATE EDITOR: **JOHN DENNING**
EDITOR, SPECIAL PROJECTS: **MARK D. BEAZLEY**
SENIOR EDITOR, SPECIAL PROJECTS: **JEFF YOUNGQUIST**
SENIOR VICE PRESIDENT OF SALES: **DAVID GABRIEL**

EDITOR IN CHIEF: **JOE QUESADA**
PUBLISHER: **DAN BUCKLEY**
EXECUTIVE PRODUCER: **ALAN FINE**

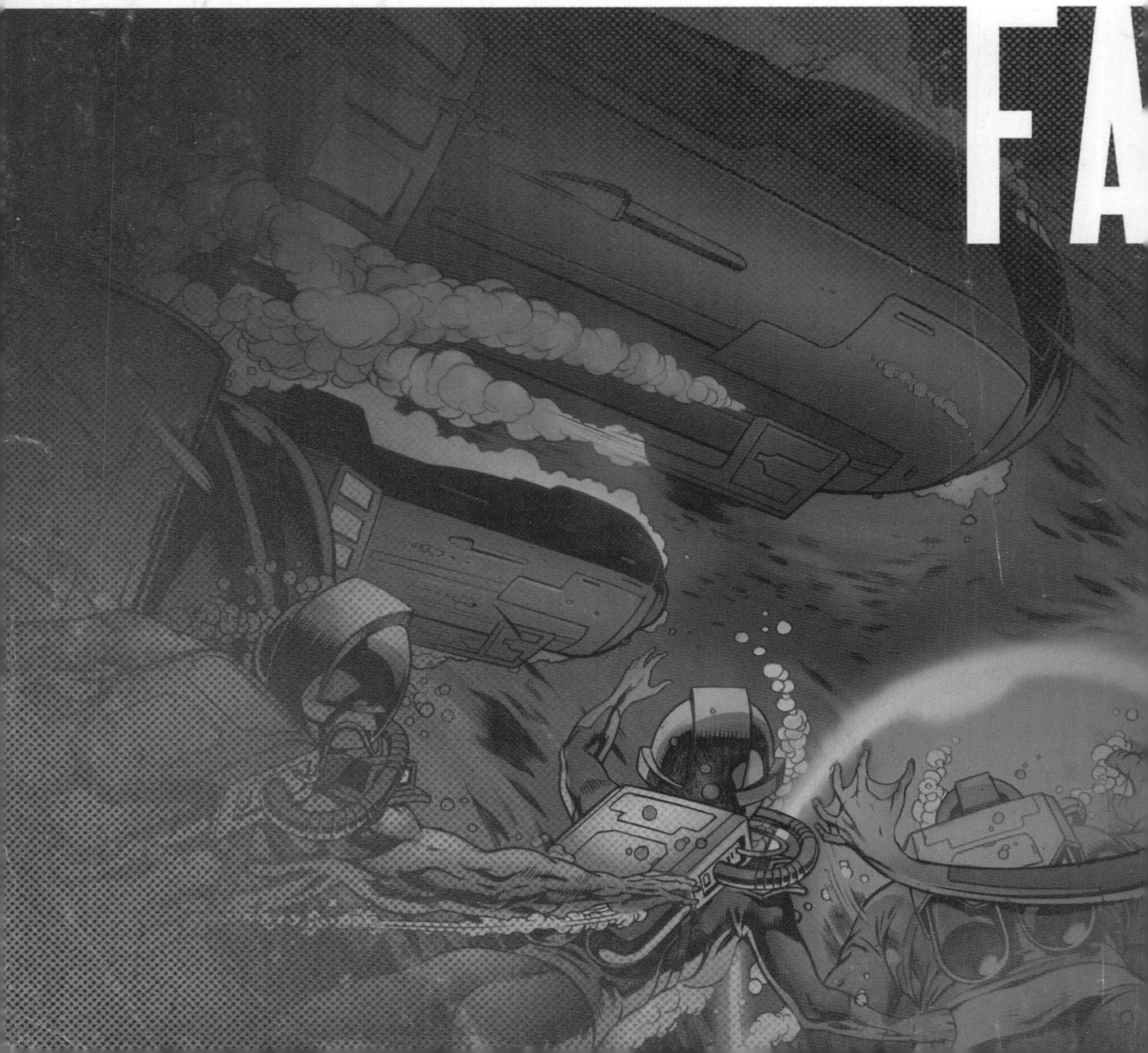
FA

NTASTIC FOUR

UNIFIED FIELD THEORY: STAN LEE & JACK KIRBY

FANTASTIC FOUR BY JONATHAN HICKMAN VOL. 2. Contains material originally published in magazine form as FANTASTIC FOUR #575-578. First printing 2010. Hardcover ISBN# 978-0-7851-4716-9. Softcover ISBN# 978-0-7851-4541-7. Published by MARVEL WORLDWIDE, INC., a subsidiary of MARVEL ENTERTAINMENT, LLC. OFFICE OF PUBLICATION: 417 5th Avenue, New York, NY 10016. Copyright © 2010 Marvel Characters, Inc. All rights reserved. Hardcover: $19.99 per copy in the U.S. and $22.50 in Canada (GST #R127032852). Softcover: $15.99 per copy in the U.S. and $17.99 in Canada (GST #R127032852). Canadian Agreement #40668537. All characters featured in this issue and the distinctive names and likenesses thereof, and all related indicia are trademarks of Marvel Characters, Inc. No similarity between any of the names, characters, persons, and/or institutions in this magazine with those of any living or dead person or institution is intended, and any such similarity which may exist is purely coincidental. **Printed in the U.S.A.** ALAN FINE, EVP - Office of the President, Marvel Worldwide, Inc. and EVP & CMO Marvel Characters B.V.; DAN BUCKLEY, Chief Executive Officer and Publisher - Print, Animation & Digital Media; JIM SOKOLOWSKI, Chief Operating Officer; DAVID GABRIEL, SVP of Publishing Sales & Circulation; DAVID BOGART, SVP of Business Affairs & Talent Management; MICHAEL PASCIULLO, VP Merchandising & Communications; JIM O'KEEFE, VP of Operations & Logistics; DAN CARR, Executive Director of Publishing Technology; JUSTIN F. GABRIE, Director of Publishing & Editorial Operations; SUSAN CRESPI, Editorial Operations Manager; ALEX MORALES, Publishing Operations Manager; STAN LEE, Chairman Emeritus. For information regarding advertising in Marvel Comics or on Marvel.com, please contact Ron Stern, VP of Business Development, at rstern@marvel.com. For Marvel subscription inquiries, please call 800-217-9158. **Manufactured between 5/17/10 and 6/16/10 (hardcover), and 5/17/10 and 11/10/10 (softcover), by R.R. DONNELLEY, INC., SALEM, VA, USA.**

10 9 8 7 6 5 4 3 2 1

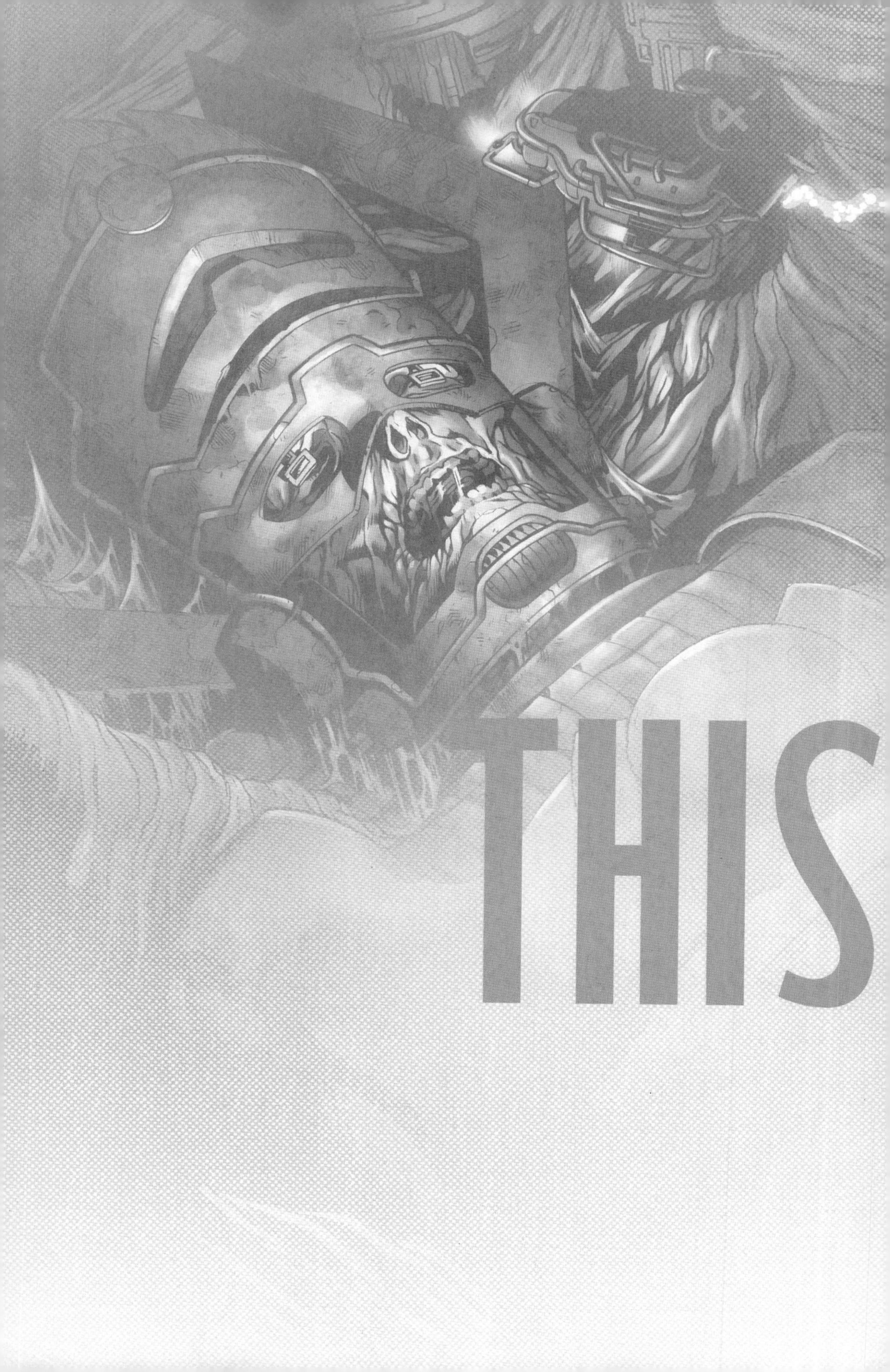
THIS

IS A
SUMMONING

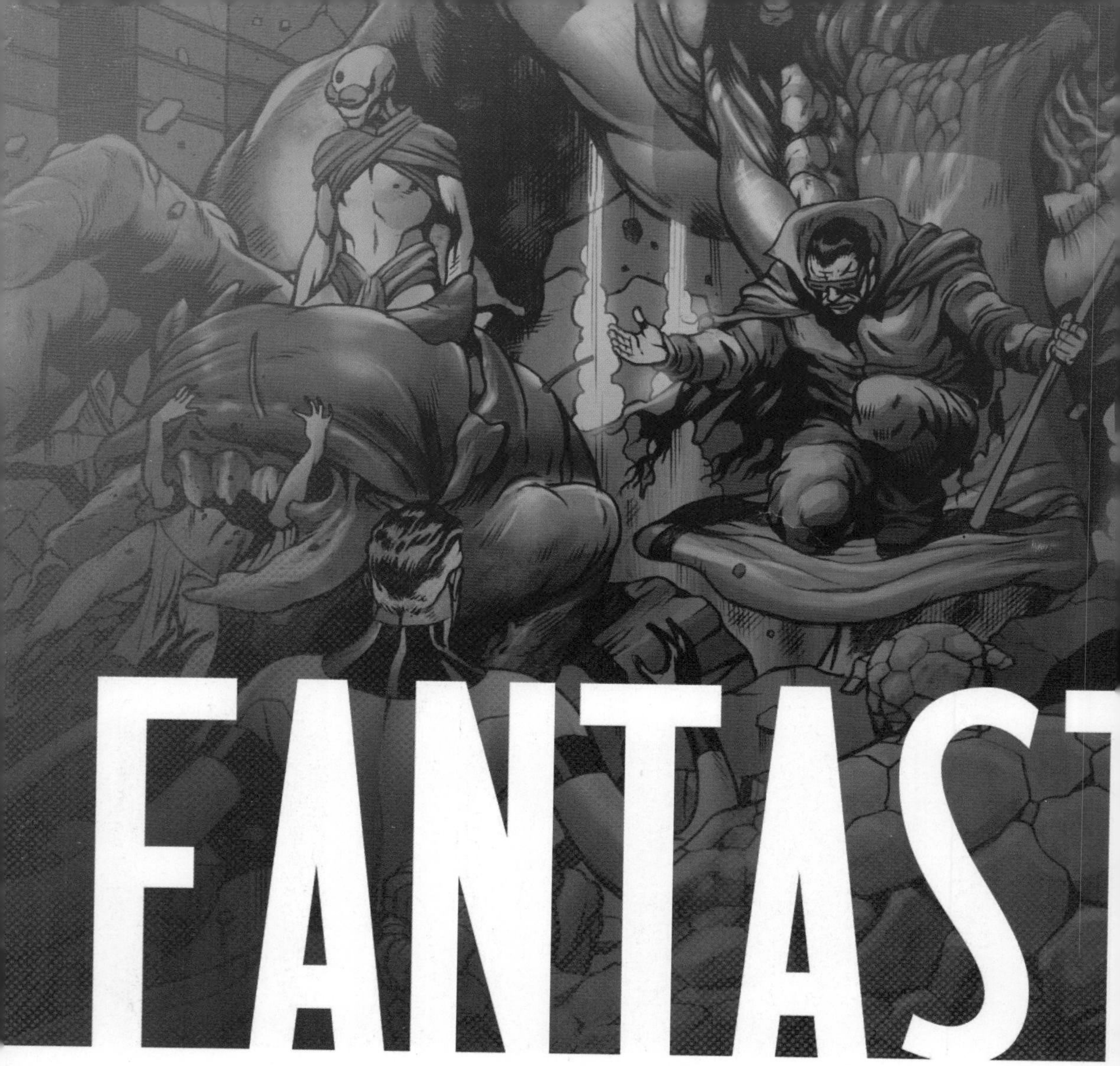
FANTAS

TIC FOUR

VOL TWO PRIME ELEMENTS

THIS CITY IT CHANGES YOU

THE BAXTER BUILDING. NEW YORK CITY.

BAAAMMM!

POP

WELCOME TO THE BAXTER BUILDING. HOME OF THE--

[H.E.R.B.I.E.]

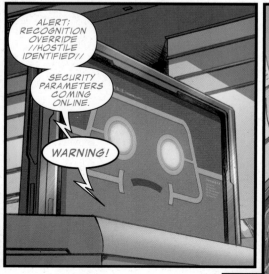

ALERT: RECOGNITION OVERRIDE //HOSTILE IDENTIFIED//

SECURITY PARAMETERS COMING ONLINE.

WARNING!

"AUTHORITY FIGURES ARE BEING ALERTED."

SECONDS LATER...

I THINK THAT'S FAR ENOUGH!

WHAT ARE YOU DOING HERE?

FANTASTIC NUMBERED FOUR...

I BRING YOU A MESSAGE FROM THE MOLE MAN.

SPIT IT OUT, BEFORE I KNOCK YOUR HEAD...

...BACK ON OR SOMETHIN'.

WELL?

PLEASE CLEAR THE LOBBY.

RRRUMMMBLE

MY OLDEST OF ADVERSARIES...

THERE IS CHAOS IN THE UNDERWORLD... SUBTERRANEA IS IN PERIL...

AND I BELIEVE YOU ARE MY ONLY HOPE.

YOU SAY THE PROBLEM IS HERE?

THIS READS AS NOTHING MORE THAN A GEOTHERMAL VENT.

IT'S DISGUISED SO THAT IT APPEARS NATURAL, BUT I ASSURE YOU, DR. RICHARDS, THE ASCENSION ENGINE THAT POWERS THE ABANDONED CITY IS MOST CERTAINLY NOT.

YOU'VE HEARD OF THE CITY, YES?

NO.

THE CITY IS THE FAILED LIFE'S WORK OF HERBERT WYNDHAM.

THE HIGH EVOLUTIONARY.

"HE BUILT A DARWIN BUBBLE. AWAY FROM THE PRYING EYES AND HYPOCRISY OF MAINSTREAM SCIENCE, HE WOULD FINALLY BE ABLE TO EXPERIMENT IN A CLOSED ENVIRONMENT AS HE WISHED...

"HE WOULD PUSH THE LIMITS OF EVOLUTIONARY SCIENCE AND THEN--TRIUMPHANT IN HIS DISCOVERY--RAISE THE CITY TO THE SURFACE FOR ALL TO SEE.

"INSTEAD OF RAPID EVOLUTION, AS IT SPUN UP, THE ASCENSION ENGINE BEGAN TO DEVOLVE THOSE WITHIN THE CITY.

"THE HIGH EVOLUTIONARY AND HIS NEW MEN WERE FORCED TO FLEE. THEY ALSO FAILED TO DEACTIVATE THE MACHINE.

IT DIDN'T WORK.

"THE CITY WAS LATER FOUND BY MY MOLOIDS. NOT KNOWING WHAT IT WAS--AND POSSESSING THE IGNORANT CURIOSITY OF LESSER CREATURES--THEY VENTURED INSIDE.

"WHO WOULD HAVE KNOWN THAT THE DEVOLVED FORM OF THE MOLOID WAS SOMETHING RESEMBLING A HUMAN BEING?

"WHO COULD HAVE GUESSED THERE WOULD BE A MORE ALARMING CHANGE?"

IF THE HIGH EVOLUTIONARY HAD REMAINED IN THE CITY UNTIL THE ENGINE COMPLETELY SPUN UP, HIS INTELLIGENCE WOULD HAVE BEEN MAGNIFIED...

INCREASED TO A SUPERHUMAN LEVEL.

FASCINATING.

IS THAT WHY YOU CAN SPEAK? IS THE CHANGE PERMANENT?

YES...FOR THOSE WHO, LIKE MYSELF, WERE BORN IN THE CITY.

I LEFT BECAUSE WE ARE CONSIDERED PARIAHS...

OUTCASTS.

THAT'S OKAY, MR. HEAD. IF YOU NEED TO, YOU CAN STAY HERE WITH US.

I HATE TO BE THAT GUY, BUT WHAT DOES ANY OF THIS HAVE TO DO WITH US?

BECAUSE, MY BOY, THEY ARE GOING TO RAISE THE CITY.

DEEP WITHIN THE AEOLUS' CAVE PASSAGE LEADING TO SUBTERRANEA. LATER.

EVERYONE GET COMFORTABLE.

THE SHIP WASN'T BUILT FOR THIS, SO THINGS COULD GET A LITTLE HAIRY.

WE COULD HAVE BURROWED STRAIGHT DOWN.

NO...DRILLING DOWN WOULD COLLAPSE THE CAVERN AND THE CITY LIES ON A FAULT LINE-- THAT COULD TRIGGER A SEISMIC EVENT, SO WE'LL TAKE A SAFER APPROACH.

AND I'VE BEEN THIS WAY BEFORE.

MY GOD... IS THAT--?

YES.

THIS IS WHERE I BURIED THE GALACTUS FROM THE FUTURE.

THIS MARKS THE EDGE OF THE UNDERWORLD.

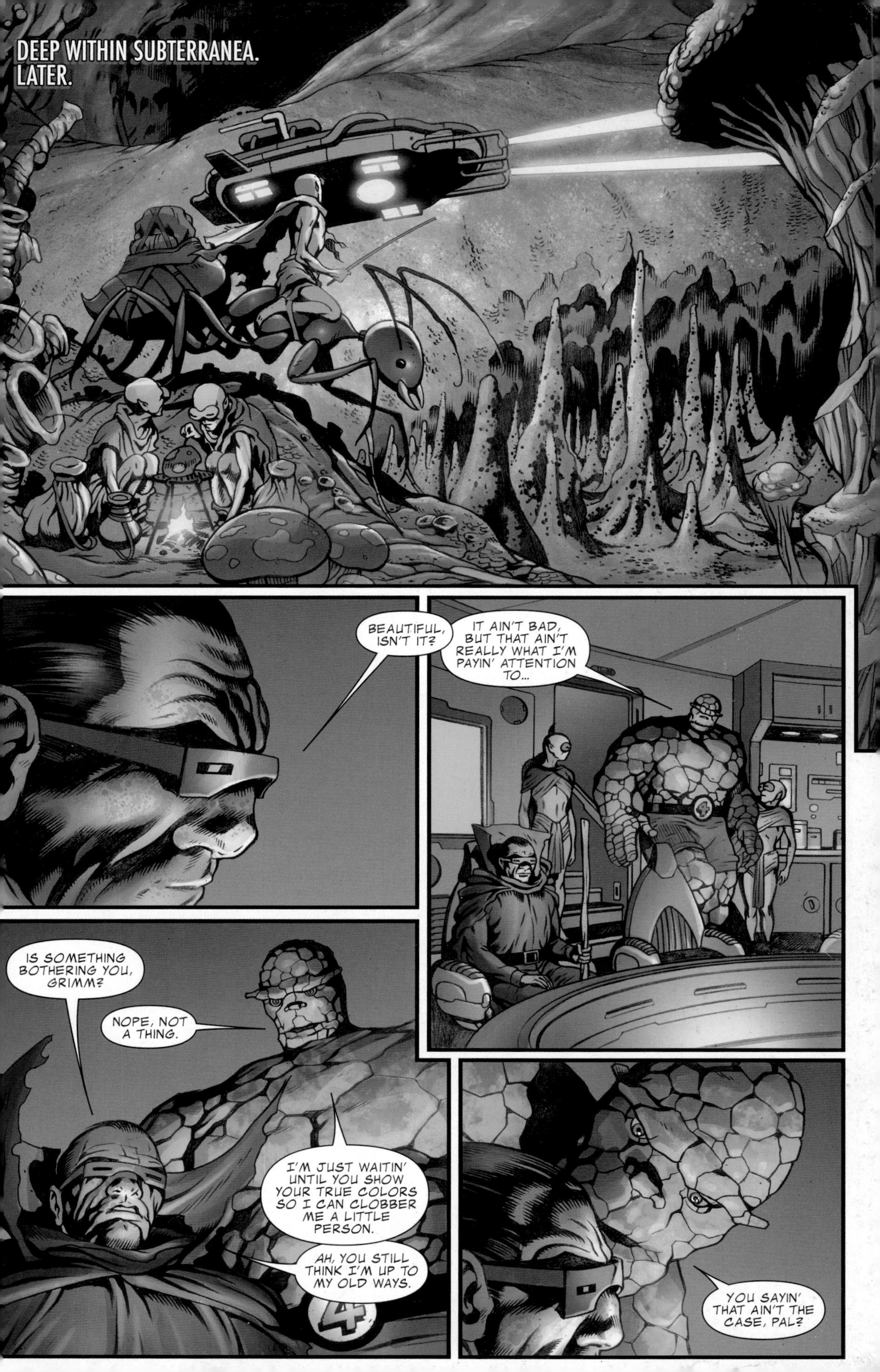

DEEP WITHIN SUBTERRANEA. LATER.
BEAUTIFUL, ISN'T IT?
IT AIN'T BAD, BUT THAT AIN'T REALLY WHAT I'M PAYIN' ATTENTION TO...
IS SOMETHING BOTHERING YOU, GRIMM?
NOPE, NOT A THING.
I'M JUST WAITIN' UNTIL YOU SHOW YOUR TRUE COLORS SO I CAN CLOBBER ME A LITTLE PERSON.
AH, YOU STILL THINK I'M UP TO MY OLD WAYS.
YOU SAYIN' THAT AIN'T THE CASE, PAL?

I NO LONGER WANT TO DESTROY SOCIETY, GRIMM... I DON'T EVEN CARE ABOUT THE SURFACE.

LOOK AT WHAT THAT PLACE HAS BECOME--THE FALL OF MAN AND THE END OF THE WORLD...

I JUST WANT MY KINGDOM, AND I WANT IT TO BE THAT...MINE.

YOU'RE TALKIN' ABOUT THE MOLOIDS GOIN' TO THIS CITY AND BECOMIN' SOMETHIN' OTHER THAN YOUR SLAVES, RIGHT?

CERTAIN CREATURES SHOULD BE CONTENT WITH WHAT THEY ARE.

NOBODY SHOULD HAVE TO BE A MONSTER THAT DON'T WANT TO BE.

HRMPH.

DID YOU KNOW THAT THE MOLOIDS IN THE CITY REFUSE TO REPRODUCE?

THEY DID AT FIRST, BUT THE PROCESS THEY UNDERWENT MADE THEIR CHILDREN LIKE THE ONE YOU MET AT THE BAXTER BUILDING...

JUST AS INTELLIGENT, BUT THEY STILL HAD THEIR OLD SKIN...A CONSTANT REMINDER OF WHAT HAS BEEN, SO THEN THEY STOPPED HAVING BABIES.

NOW, THEY ONLY GROW THEIR NUMBERS BY ABSORBING MY PEOPLE INTO THE CITY.

"DO YOU KNOW WHAT THEY DID WITH THOSE CHILDREN? THEY ABANDONED THEM IN THE AREA UNDERNEATH THE CITY.

"THEY LEFT THEM TO SURVIVE ALL ALONE... NOW, THERE ARE ONLY A FEW LEFT.

"SO I ASK YOU--WHICH IS BETTER...?"

SIMPLE CREATURE WHO KNOW NOTHIN MORE THAN COMMUNITY AND THE COMFORT O THEIR FAMILY, O ENLIGHTENED INDIVIDUALS WHO ABANDON THOSE THINGS FOR THEIR OWN PERSONAL GAIN?

HUH? WE'VE STOPPED.

IS THIS THE END OF THE LINE?

OH, NO... WE'LL BE GOING MUCH DEEPER.

"INTO THE CAVERN CITY OF *LECHUGUILLA*...

"BENEATH THAT, THROUGH THE UNDERWATER CITY OF MERAMEC...

"TO OUR FINAL DESTINATION."

THERE. THERE IT IS...

THE GATES OF THE ABANDONED CITY OF THE HIGH EVOLUTIONARY.

WE'RE TOO LATE.

THE CITY HAS ALREADY BEGUN TO RISE.

THIS ENTIRE CAVERN IS GOING TO COLLAPSE.

WE HAVE TO GET OUT OF HERE.

BEN, WHAT ARE YOU...

STICK AROUND AS LONG AS YOU CAN.

WAIT, BEN... STOP!

SOMETHIN' I GOTTA DO.

SORRY, STRETCH...

URK! What's happenin'?

THIS CITY...IT CHANGES YOU.

Where are the children?

WE KEEP THE ANIMALS IN THEIR PENS...

ON THE UNDERSIDE OF THE CITY.

SMASH!

Where is everyone else?

WE'RE ALL THAT'S LEFT.

C'mon...

I'm gettin' you outta here.

HERE THEY COME.

GOOD THING, BECAUSE THE ENTIRE ROOF IS GETTING READY TO COME DOWN!

BEN! WHAT HAPPENED TO...

Later, Suzie... Kids, buckle yourselves in tight.

Reed! Let's go!

WHERE ARE WE GOING TO GO...THE WORLD IS CAVING IN ON...

OH!

REED! LOOK!

MAYBE...

SUE, YOU'RE GOING TO NEED TO SHIELD US.

HERE WE GO.

LATER.

THE MOLE MAN LEFT?

YES. A WHILE AGO... HE SLITHERED BACK BENEATH THE EARTH TO RALLY WHAT'S LEFT OF HIS KINGDOM, I'M SURE.

THIS REALLY IS AMAZING...

WHAT WE THOUGHT WOULD CRACK THE EARTH WAS INSTEAD DESIGNED TO SEAL BEHIND ITSELF, CREATING A SOLID FOUNDATION BENEATH THE CITY AS IT ROSE.

SO, WHAT'S GOING TO HAPPEN NOW?

I'M NOT SURE... ACCUSATIONS, FEAR...POLITICS. NO DOUBT WE'LL BE INVOLVED.

REGARDLESS, THEY'RE HERE TO STAY.

I'M JUST SAYIN'...

Reed says it'll take an hour or so to wear off.

SERIOUSLY, DON'T DISMISS THIS--PEOPLE LOVE MONKEYS... AND IT'S A GOOD LOOK FOR YOU.

Shut up.

DID YOU GET THE CHILDREN SETTLED?

Yeah...

But there's somethin' funny about those kids.

AND WHAT ABOUT THEIR INTENTIONS?

THEY HAVE AN INHUMAN PERSPECTIVE AND AN UNNATURAL LEVEL OF INTELLIGENCE, BEN...

THEY ARE A PRODUCT OF THEIR CITY.

I WOULDN'T WORRY ABOUT IT, THEY'RE NOT SO SPECIAL THAT WE WON'T BE ABLE TO HANDLE THEM IF THEY'RE UP TO NO GOOD.

STILL...A MAN-MADE CITY RAISED FROM DEEP WITHIN THE EARTH, RUN BY SUPER-GENIUS DEVOLVED MONSTERS...YOU DON'T SEE THAT EVERY DAY.

Yeah...

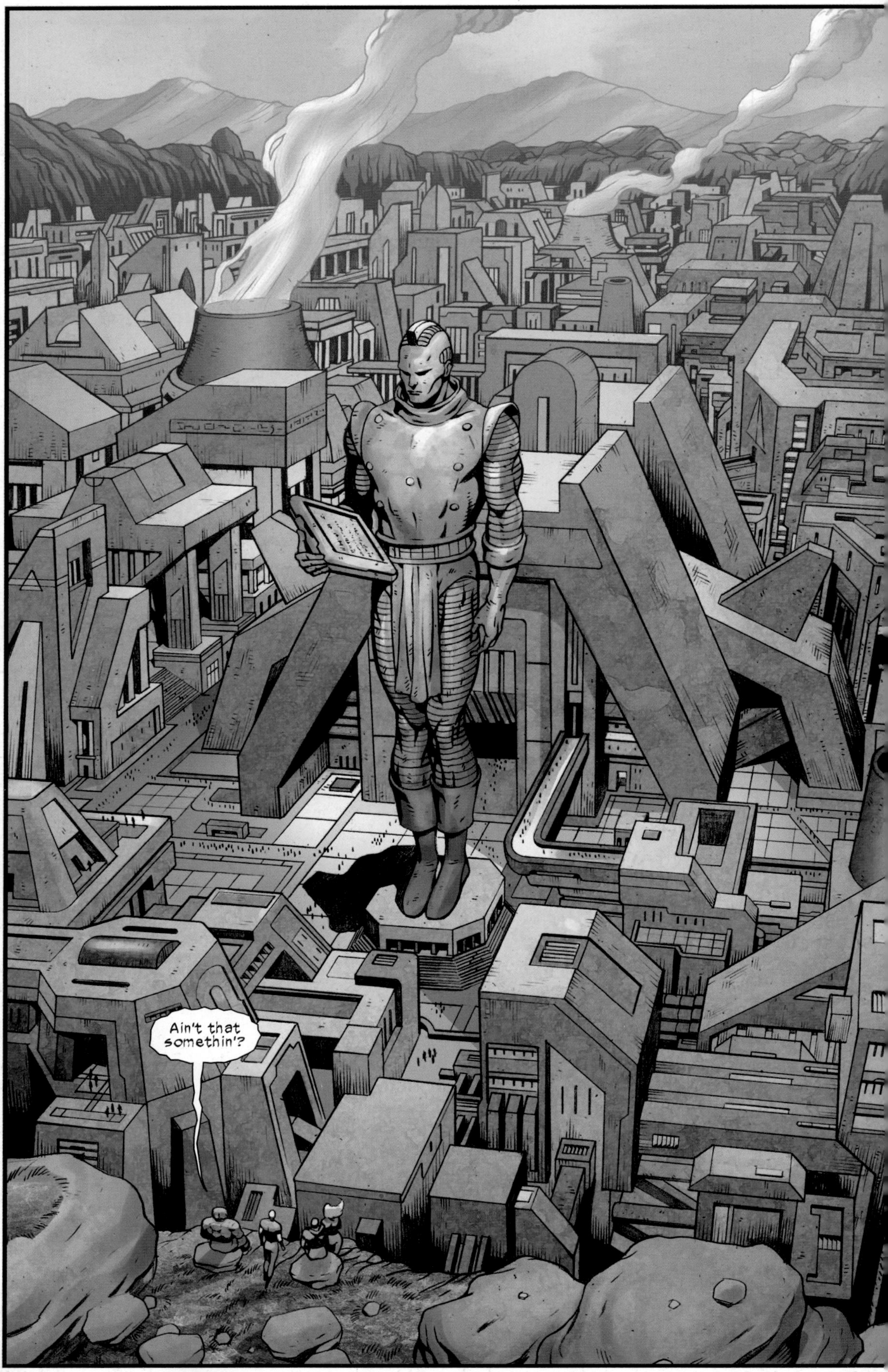
Ain't that somethin'?

- ONE HOUR AND TWENTY-THREE MINUTES AFTER LEAVING THE CITY, BEN GRIMM REVERTED TO HIS NON-DEVOLVED STATE.

- EXPERIMENTATION CONDUCTED ON THE EDGE OF THE CITY SUGGESTS THAT LEVEL A CONTAINMENT SUITS WILL PREVENT THE EFFECTS OF THE HIGH EVOLUTIONARY'S ASCENSION ENGINE.

- FOUR DAYS AFTER RISING, DIPLOMATIC ENVOYS FROM THE UNITED STATES GOVERNMENT OPENED A DIALOGUE WITH THE "FOREVER CITY OF THE HIGH EVOLUTIONARY" REGARDING TERRITORIAL RIGHTS.

  NEGOTIATIONS BROKE DOWN OVER THE DEMAND FROM FOREVER CITY AMBASSADORS THAT IT BE TREATED AS AN INDEPENDENT NATION-STATE WITHIN THE CONTINENTAL U.S. BORDER.

  CHECKPOINTS WERE CONSTRUCTED TO RESTRICT ACCESS UNTIL A RESOLUTION ACCEPTABLE TO BOTH PARTIES CAN BE REACHED. MEDIATION CONTINUES.

- AFTER TWO WEEKS, THE MOLOID CHILDREN WHO WERE RESCUED FROM THE CITY SHOW NO SIGNS OF DIMINISHED INTELLIGENCE.

homepad

WHERE THERE IS **WATER** AND **LIFE** LIVED IN IT THERE ARE **GIANTS**

OKAY...I KNOW IT'S TOUGH TO FOCUS WITH SUPER-SMART OLOID KIDS RUNNING AROUND AND DIGGING INTO EVERYTHING...

BUT PAY ATTENTION, BOYS... OR I'LL SEND YOU TO THE CORNER.

THIS IS VOSTOK STATION.

A RESEARCH FACILITY BUILT BY RUSSIAN EXPLORERS IN THE 1950S. ITS ONLY REMARKABLE TRAIT BEING THAT IT WAS THE MOST ISOLATED BASE IN ALL OF ANTARCTICA.

THE ONLY HOTSPOT IN A COLD AND UNFORGIVING PLACE.

JUMP FORWARD TO 1973 WHEN RADAR IMAGING REVEALED THE LARGEST SUSPENDED BODY OF WATER IN THE ENTIRE CONTINENT SOME 13,000 FEET BENEATH THE SURFACE.

IT'S MASSIVE. BEST ESTIMATES SHOW THE AREA TO BE SOMEWHERE AROUND 6,000 SQUARE MILES. MUCH MORE INTERESTING THAN THAT...*THE POINT* REALLY, IS LAKE VOSTOK HAS BEEN AN ISOLATED HABITAT FOR OVER 500,000 YEARS.

ANY LIFE THAT MAY HAVE FORMED THERE WILL HAVE FOLLOWED A DIVERGENT, BUT PARALLEL, EVOLUTIONARY PATH FROM OUR OWN.

FOR DECADES, BIOLOGISTS AND GEOLOGISTS TRIED, UNSUCCESSFULLY, TO EXPLORE THIS AREA WITH TRADITIONAL METHODS AND EQUIPMENT.

BUT OUTSIDE OF SOME IMPRESSIVE ICE CORE SAMPLES AND INTERESTING THERMAL DATA, THEY HAD NOTHING TO SHOW FOR THEIR EFFORTS.

THEN, FOUR YEARS AGO, A SELECT GROUP OF SCIENTISTS WON A GRANT FROM OUR PRIMARY RESEARCH FOUNDATION AND REED PROVIDED THEM WITH SOME NEXT GENERATION SCANNING EQUIPMENT-- MAKING HIGH-RESOLUTION MAPPING OF THE UNDERGROUND LAKE FROM THE SURFACE POSSIBLE.

AND, AFTER USING IT, THEY FOUND SOMETHING FASCINATING: THERE'S SOME KIND OF SUPERSTRUCTURE AT THE HEART OF LAKE VOSTOK.

AS YOU CAN IMAGINE, AFTER THAT, WE REALLY GOT INVOLVED.

WE BEGAN WHAT WE THOUGHT WAS A METHODICAL AND SYSTEMATIC PLAN FOR SAFELY LAUNCHING A SERIES OF DEEP WATER PROBES BEFORE EVENTUALLY SENDING A MANNED EXPLORATORY TEAM DOWN THERE.

BECAUSE, YOU KNOW, SLOW AND STEADY...

RIGHT! STEADY LIKE A ROCK!

NO, YOU IDIOT... TURTLE.

SLOW AND STEADY LIKE THE TURTLE.

WINS.

THE.

RACE.

IT'S SLOW AND STEADY WINS THE RACE.

FORGET IT. MOVING ON.

JUST CUT TO THE CHASE, SUZIE... TELL US WHY WE'RE HERE.

SOMETHING'S COME UP.

LAST WEEK, I NOTICED A DATA LEAK ON OUR REMOTE MAINFRAME AND DISCOVERED A.I.M. HAD CRACKED OUR SYSTEMS IN ANTARCTICA.

SO WE RE-TASKED A SATELLITE AND DISCOVERED THAT THEY HAD SECRETLY BEEN SLANT DRILLING FROM A LOCATION FIVE MILES AWAY. THEY WANT WHATEVER IS DOWN THERE AS WELL...

AND THEY ARE PREPARING TO LAUNCH EXPLORATORY VEHICLES IN THE NEXT TWENTY-FOUR HOURS.

MEANING THAT IF WE WANT TO GET THERE FIRST, OUR SCIENCE TEAM AT THE SOUTH POLE NO LONGER HAS THE LUXURY OF SENDING DOWN PROBES...

THIS IS GOING TO HAVE TO BE A MANNED MISSION FROM THE GET-GO...

...AND I VOLUNTEERED US.

WHY?

BECAUSE IS THERE ANYTHING WE DO BETTER THAN EXPLORATION?

BEAT PEOPLE UP?

DATE HOT WOMEN?

WE LEAVE IN FORTY-FIVE MINUTES.

CRASH

FOUR HOURS LATER.

DID SOMEONE ORDER PIZZA?

THE DISCOVERY BUILDING. FUTURE FOUNDATION. VOSTOK EXPLORATORY STATION [PROJECT 2B].

HELLO, DOCTOR.

IT'S GOOD TO SEE YOU AGAIN, SUSAN.

REED, THIS IS DR. CALVIN COOLEY. CAL, THIS IS MY HUSBAND, REED.

HI.

IT'S AN HONOR, DR. RICHARDS. I WANT TO THANK YOU FOR PROVIDING ALL OF THIS.

NO, NO...DON'T THANK ME. I'M ALWAYS IN THE LAB COMING UP WITH THE NEXT THING. IT'S SUSAN WHO HANDLES ALL THE DAY-TO-DAY RUNNING OF THE FOUNDATION.

YOU KNOW, I REALLY DON'T GET OUT ENOUGH... THIS IS A VERY COOL PLACE YOU'VE GOT HERE.

YES, IT IS...HOW MUCH LONGER UNTIL WE CAN LAUNCH, CAL?

OH, WE'RE READY NOW...

BUT THERE ARE A COUPLE OF THINGS THAT CONCERN US.

THE POD WILL HAVE TO BREAK THROUGH AN ICE SHIELD TO REACH THE LAKE. THIS IS WITHIN ITS STRUCTURAL LIMITS, BUT IT'S TWO THINGS HITTING EACH OTHER AT HIGH SPEED, SO IT'S GOT US A BIT ANXIOUS.

WHAT'S REALLY GOT US WORRIED IS THE MASSIVE THERMAL VENT DOWN THERE-- IT'S GOING TO BE LOUD.

WAY TOO LOUD FOR YOU TO EFFECTIVELY COMMUNICATE WITH YOUR HEADGEAR AND THERE'S NO TIME FOR A WORK-AROUND.

WE THINK YOU SHOULD SCRAP THE MISSION--THE CONDITIONS ARE TOO DANGEROUS...

BUT IT'S YOUR MONEY AND YOU GOING DOWN THERE...SO IT'S YOUR CALL, SUSAN.

LET'S GO FOR A SWIM.

30 MINUTES LATER.

82.25 METERS PER SECOND. UPPER LIMIT OF RATE OF DESCENT ACHIEVED. APPROACHING ICE SHIELD.

IMPACT IN THREE... TWO...

CRASH!!

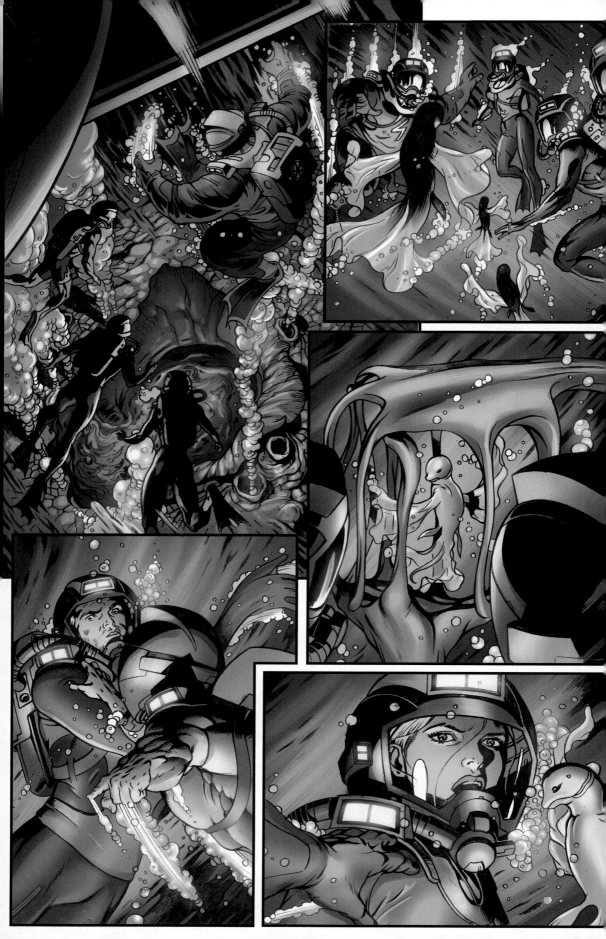

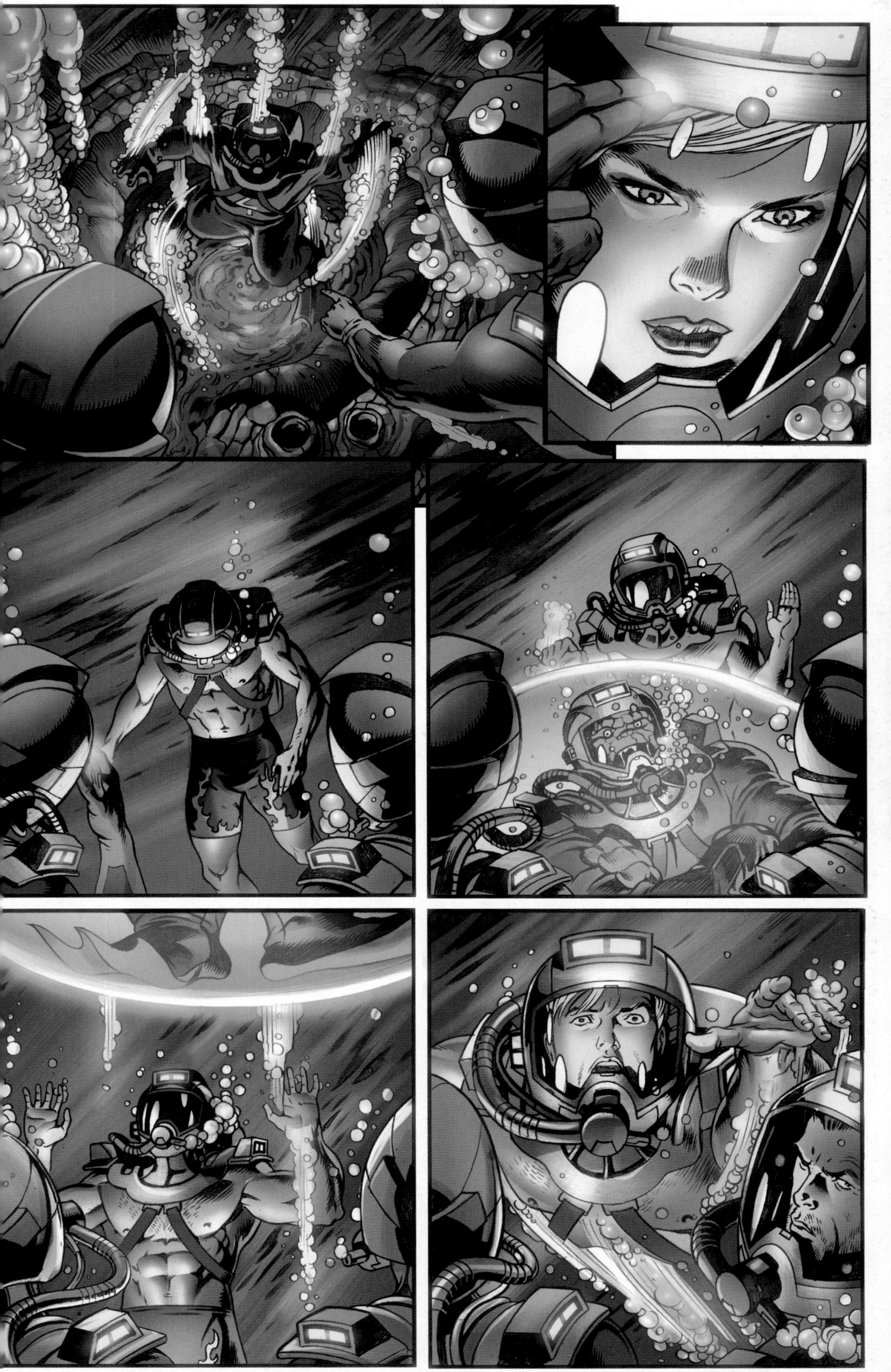

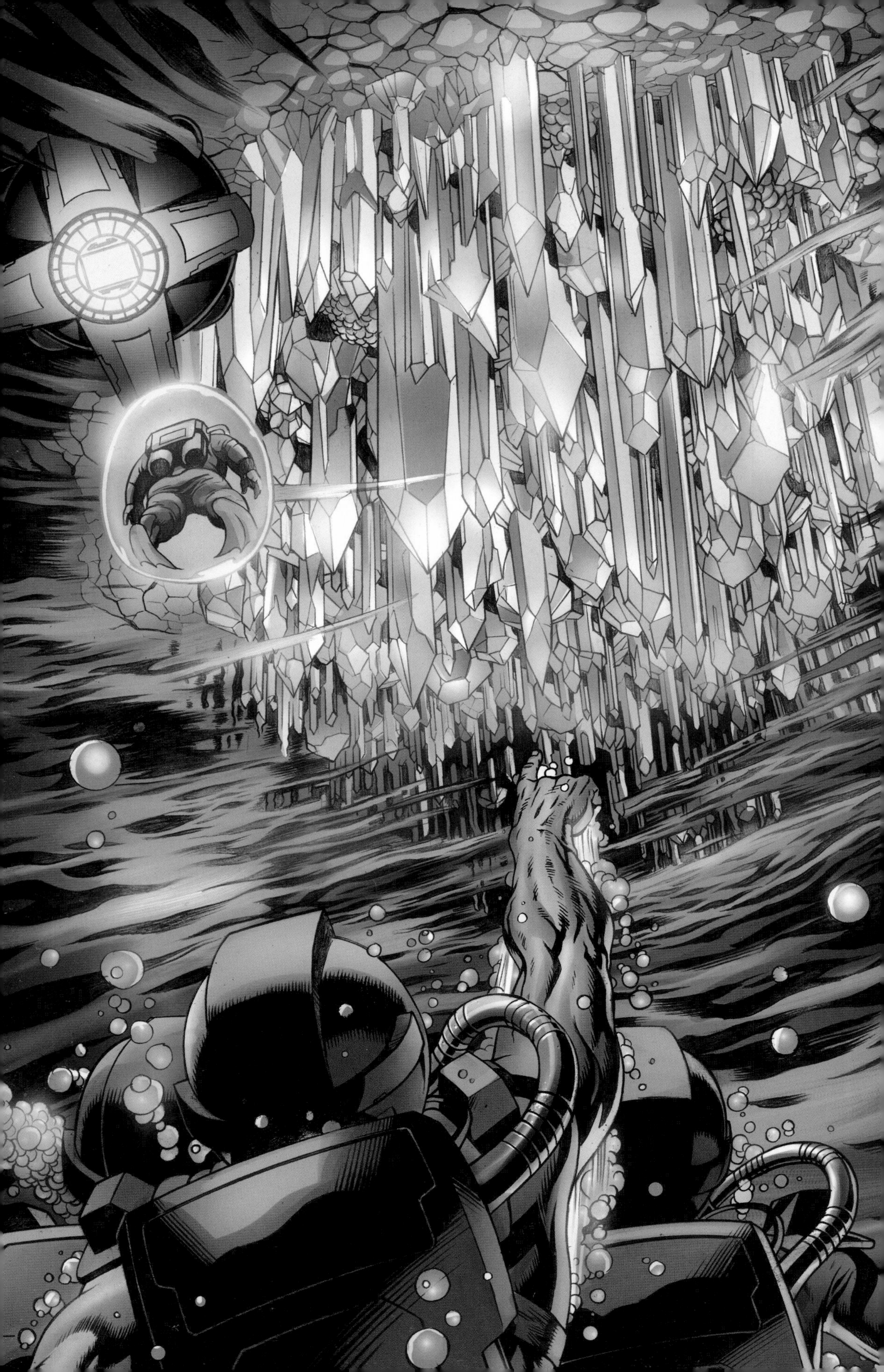

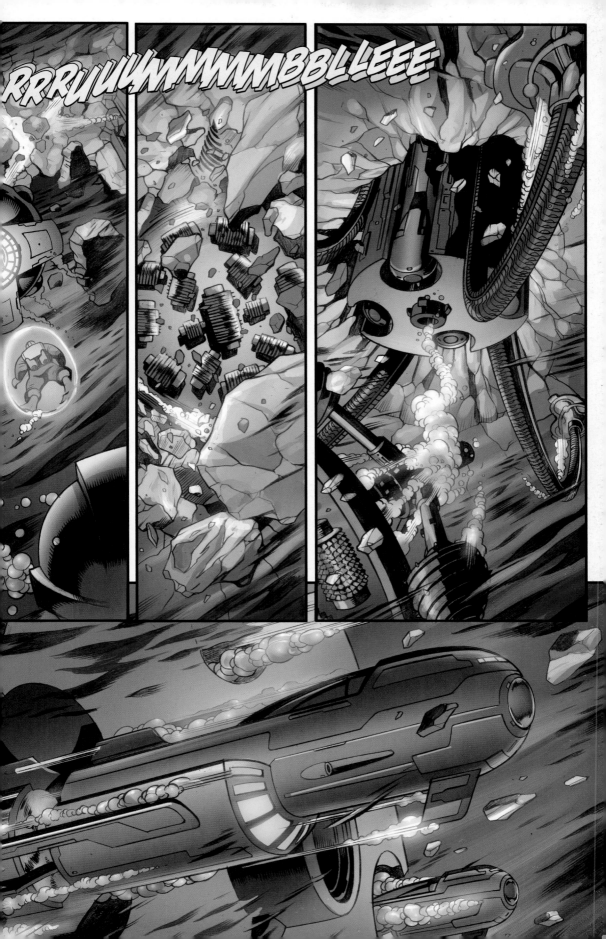

RRRUUUWWWMMMBBLLEEE-

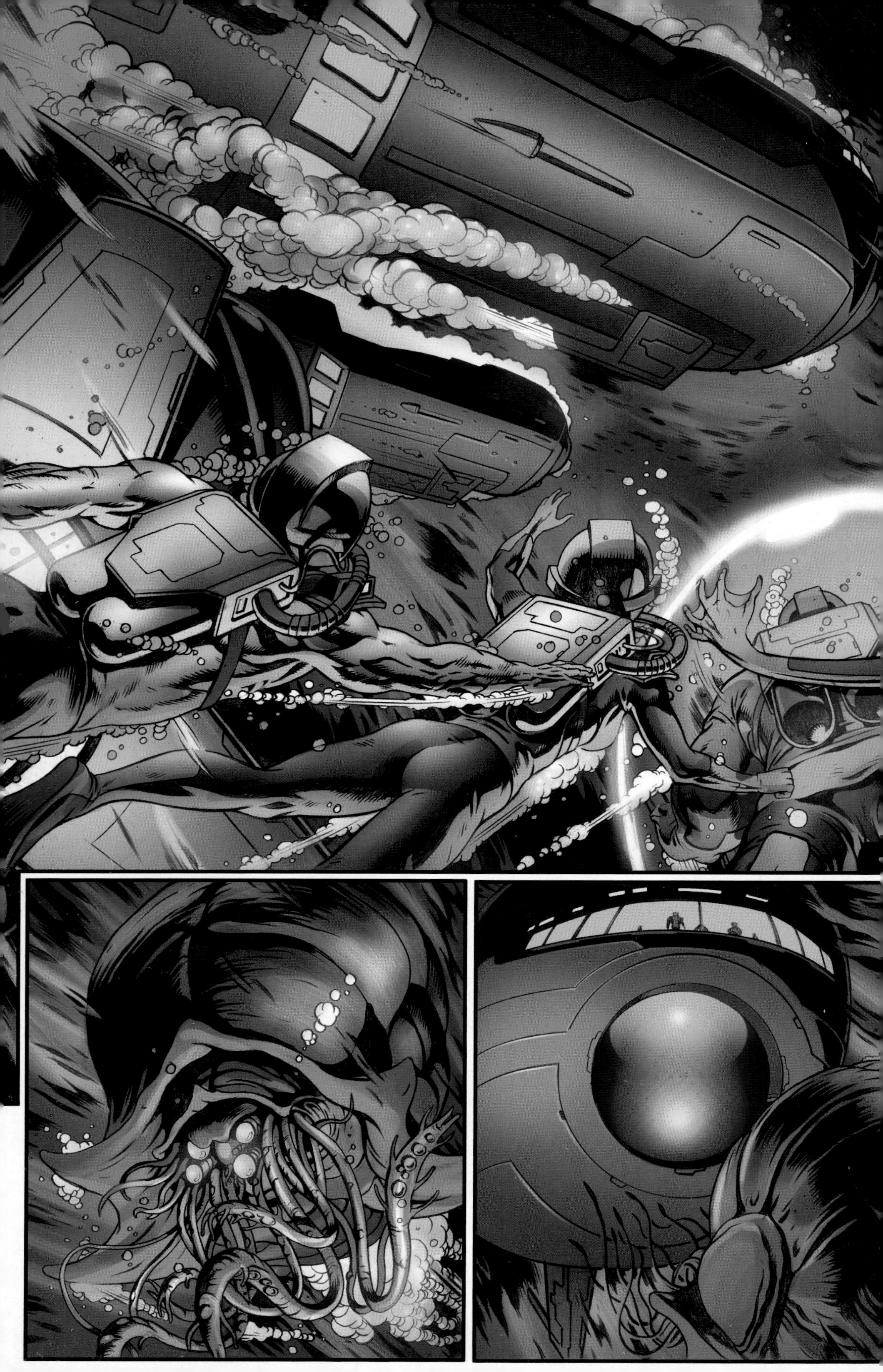

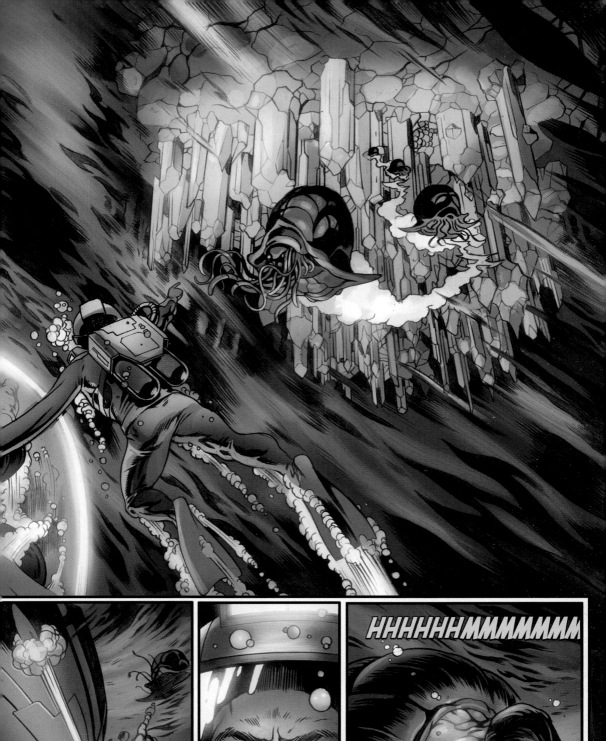

BA-BOOM

HHHHHHMMMMMMM

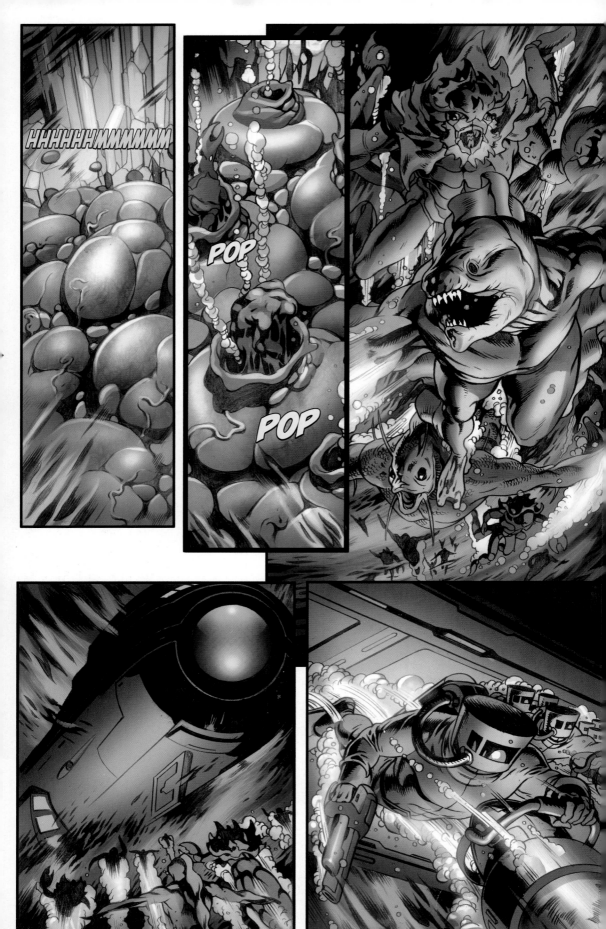

HHHHHHMMMMMM

POP

POP

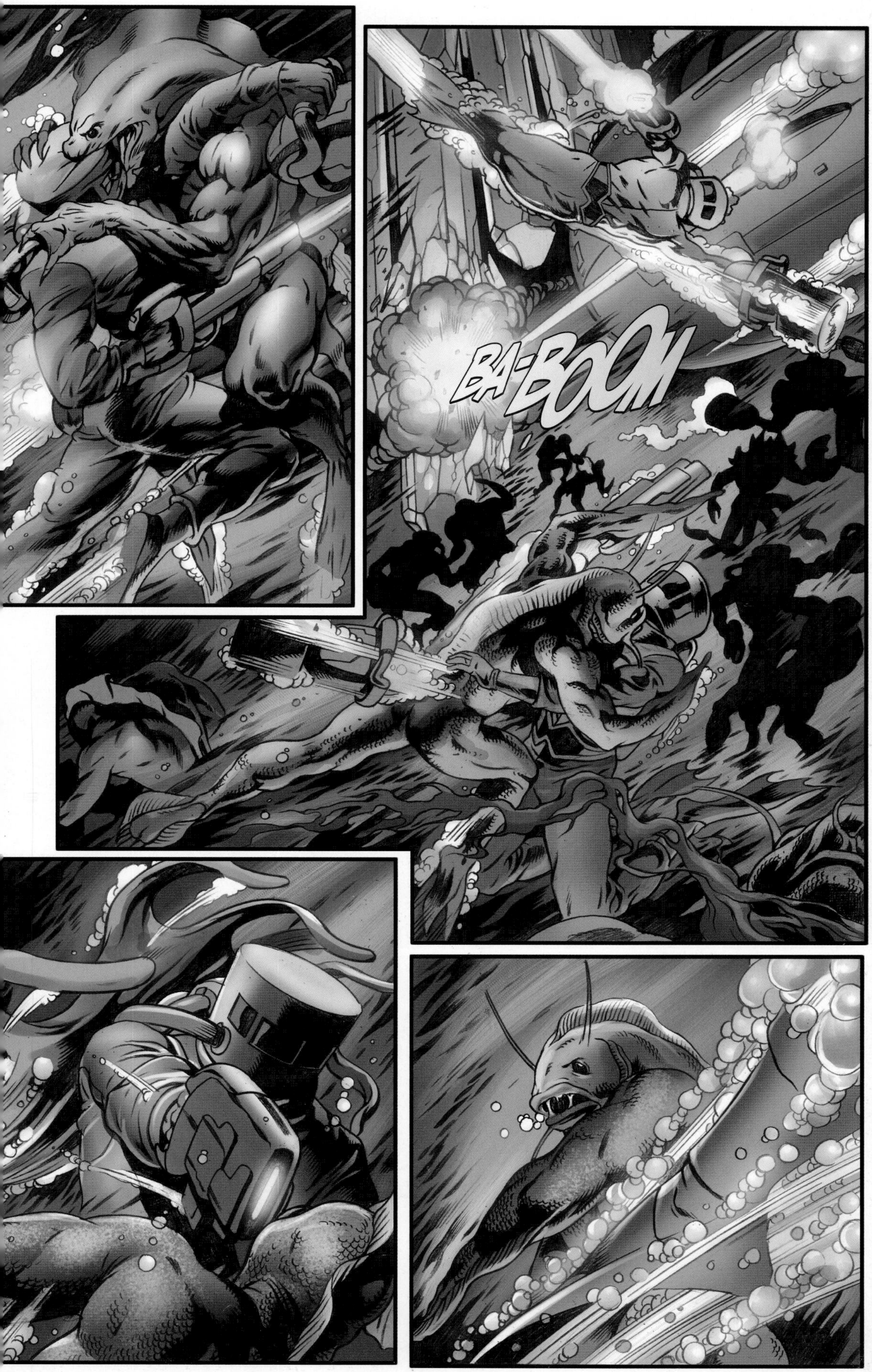
BA-BOOM

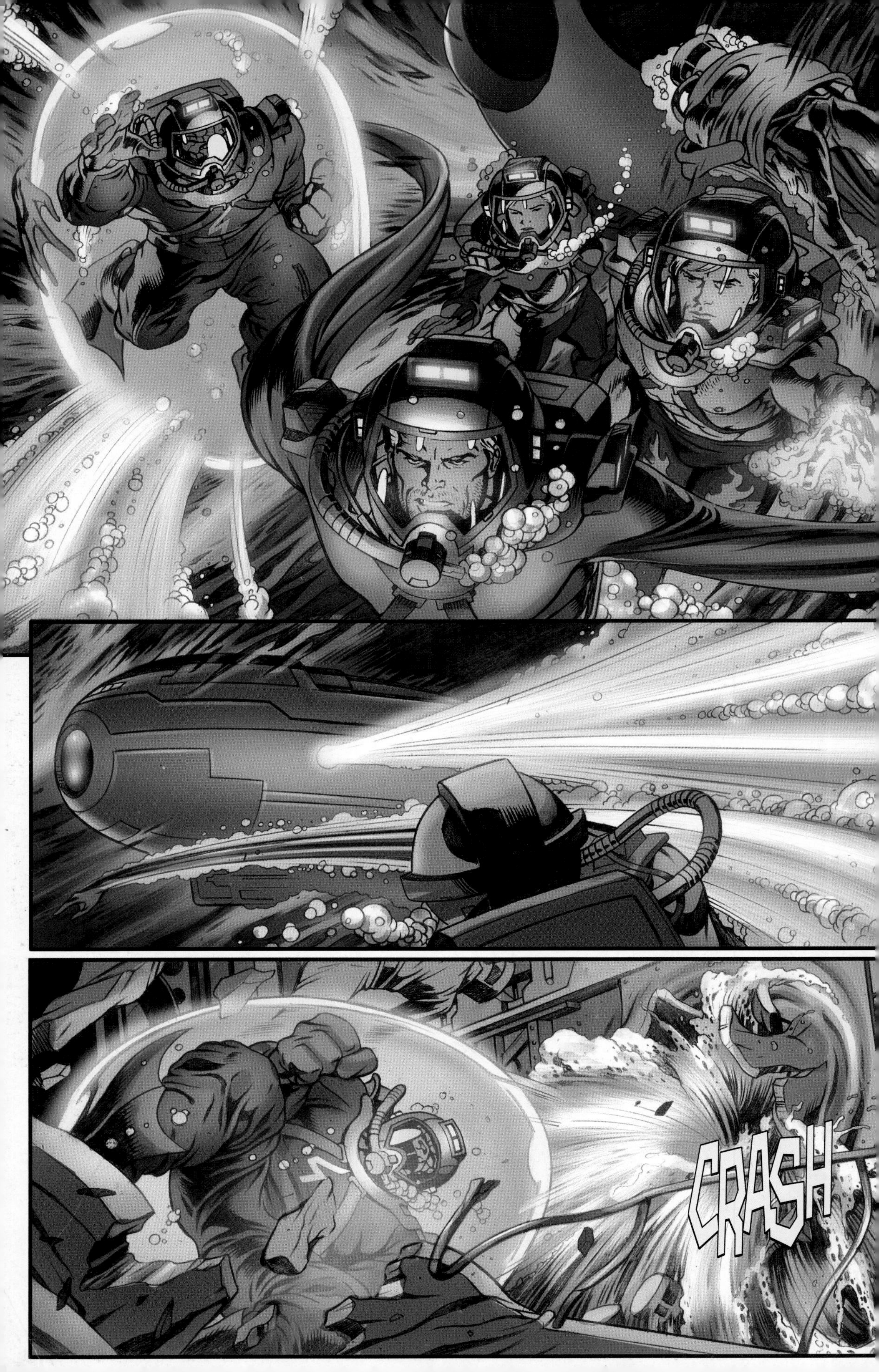
CRASH

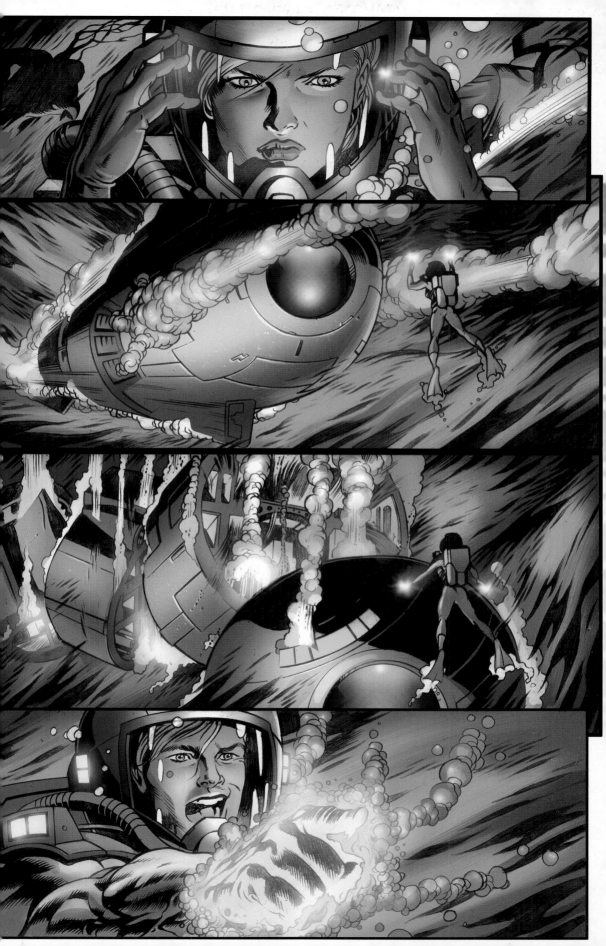

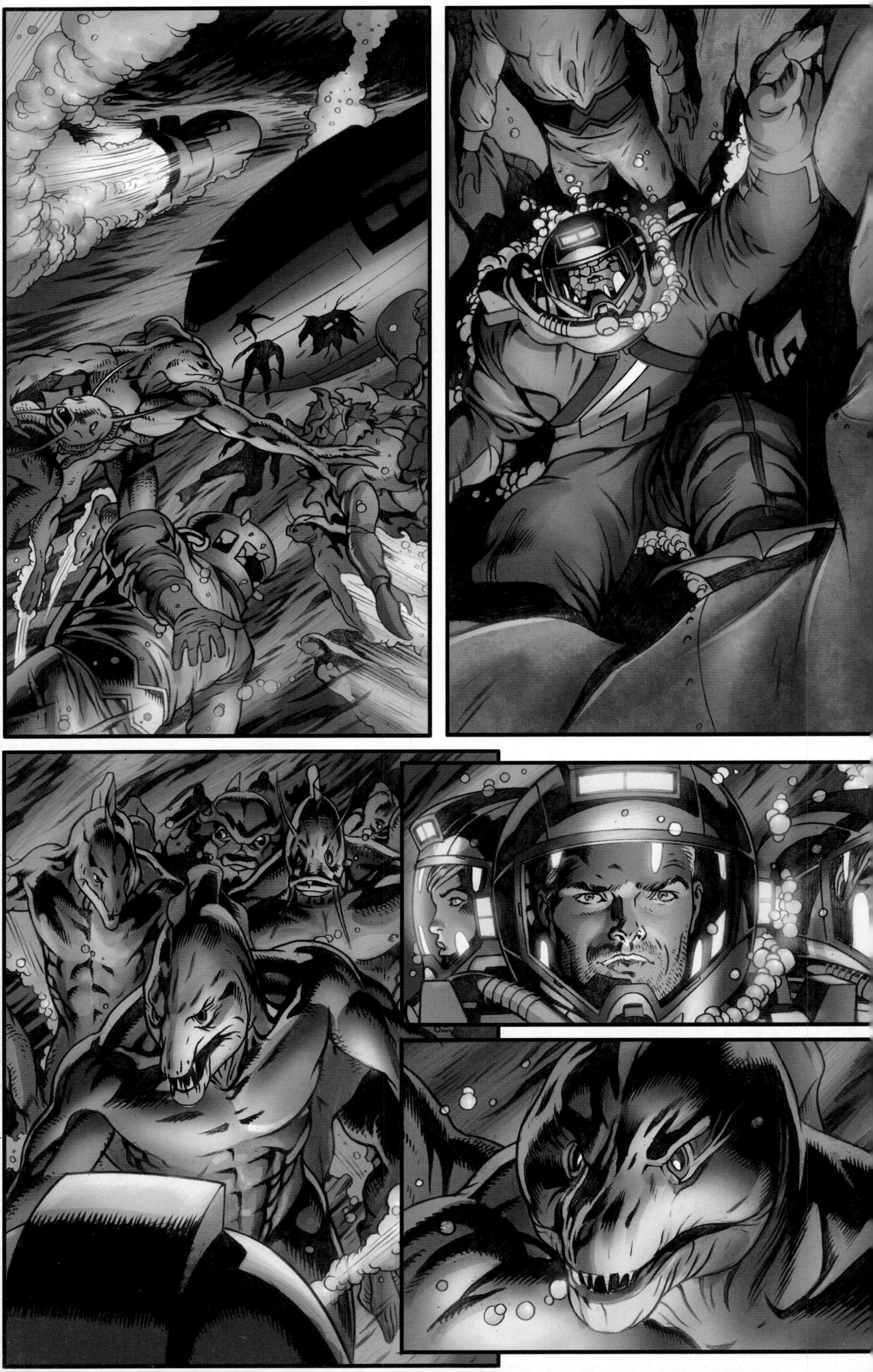

AMAZING...

IT'S SOME KIND OF TELEPATHIC COMMUNICATION DEVICE.

DON'T CARE.

I LOOK RIDICULOUS.

MORE RIDICULOUS...

YOU LOOK MORE RIDICULOUS.

SO...WHERE DO YOU THINK THEY'RE...

...TAKING US?

IT'S LIKE THE WORLD'S BIGGEST SUSHI BAR.

THAT IS **NOT A** GOOD LOOK, PAL.

HEY, JOHNNY... ROYALTY.

BRING THEM FORWARD.

I AM UL-UHAR, REGENT OF THE PEAK. KING OF THE UHARI.

WELCOME TO THE KINGDOM OF ATLANTIS.

ATLANTIS? THIS ISN'T ATLANTIS, IT'S DESTROYED... RUINS AT THE BOTTOM OF THE WORLD.

ATLANTIS IS THE SEA, BOY.

WHERE THERE IS WATER AND LIFE LIVED IN IT, THERE ARE GIANTS.

THIS IS SIMPLY THE WAY THINGS ARE.

BUT WE ARE CONFUSED. YOU BOTH CAME FROM ABOVE.

YOU...AND THEY...ARE THE SAME.

YET THEY CAME HERE TO DO VIOLENCE AND YOU TRIED TO STOP THEM. HOW IS THIS POSSIBLE?

I DON'T UNDERSTAND.

YOU SEE EVIDENCE OF THREE RACES BEFORE YOU. THE ONLY THREE THAT SURVIVED THE GREAT FALL.

WE EACH HAVE OUR OWN CULTURES... WE EACH HAVE OUR OWN RULERS. BUT AT TIMES--TIMES LIKE THESE--ONE PERSON HAS THE AUTHORITY TO SPEAK FOR ALL.

SO, I REPRESENT THE KINGDOM AND ALL ITS PEOPLE--IF NOT YOU, THEN TELL ME, WHO SPEAKS FOR MAN?

NO. THAT'S SIMPLY NOT HOW OUR SOCIETY WORKS. WHAT YOU ARE TALKING ABOUT--THAT ROLE--DOESN'T EXIST. HUMANITY IS NOT A COLLECTIVE.

THERE ISN'T A SINGLE...WHAT I'M SAYING IS THAT NO ONE WOULD EVER...

I WILL.

WHAT?!

I WILL BE THE VOICE OF MAN.

SUSAN, IT'S NOT YOUR...

IT'S WHAT THEY UNDERSTAND...

AND YOU KNOW WHY IT HAS TO BE ME.

COME FORWARD AND TELL US WHO YOU ARE.

I AM SUSAN STORM RICHARDS.

AND NOW, SO MUCH MORE.

SUSAN OF THE RICHARDS, SUSAN OF THE STORM... ENVOY OF MAN AND EMISSARY OF THE PEAK.

RETURN FROM WHERE YOU CAME, AND SPREAD THE WORD...

THE *OLD KINGS* OF ATLANTIS HAVE RETURNED.

IF EVER WE ARE NEEDED, IF EVER THERE IS CAUSE FOR CONTACT, THERE IS ONE PERSON WITH WHOM THEY NEED SPEAK.

AND IN THESE HALLS, HER NAME WILL ALWAYS ECHO OUT.

I AM SUSAN RICHARDS.

AND I SPEAK FOR ALL MANKIND.

- BEFORE LEAVING THE PEAK, SUSAN RICHARDS WAS GIVEN AN ACCESS DEVICE -- THE SPIRAL -- TO BE USED IF COMMUNICATION WAS DESIRED BY EITHER PARTY.

- THE OLD KINGDOM IS SUPPORTED BY A HYDRO-DYNAMIC APPARATUS POWERED BY LAKE VOSTOK'S INTERNAL CURRENT, WHICH IS A RESULT OF THE ICE SHELF ABOVE AND THE THERMAL VENT BELOW.

- THE THREE RACES THAT EXIST IN THE OLD KINGDOM ARE THE UHARI (FISH-LIKE IN APPEARANCE), THE CHORDAI (EEL-LIKE IN APPEARANCE), AND THE MALA (CRAB-LIKE IN APPEARANCE).

  TRADITIONALLY, THE UHARI ARE A WORKER CLASS, THE MALA ARE A LEGAL CLASS, AND THE CHORDAI ARE A WARRIOR CLASS.

- SOON AFTER LEAVING ANTARCTICA, SUSAN RICHARDS TOOK THE FIRST STEPS TOWARDS ACHIEVING WHAT SHE HOPED WOULD BE A PEACEFUL ASSEMBLY OF ALL UNDERSEA CULTURES BY CONTACTING KING NAMOR VIA UTOPIA.

  NAMOR HAS YET TO RESPOND.

homepad

BUT THE
SUPREMOR
YOU SEE... HE HAD
OTHER PLANS

SIX MONTHS AGO.
THE BLUE AREA OF THE MOON.

IT IS TIME.

WHAT FOLLOWS WILL BE A DELICATE PERIOD--*ALL THINGS* LIE IN FLUX.

EVEN AS THE TIME OF *GATHERING* DRAWS NEAR, CIRCUMSTANCES FORCE US AWAY... SO SOMEONE MUST STAY BEHIND

OF ALL *INHUMANS,* YOU WERE CHOSEN.

I AM YOUR WAYFINDER, MY LORD.

BLACK BOLT HAS A SAYING. MAY NEVER A WORD BE UTTERED WHEN ACTION ALONE WILL DO.

THIS IS A SUMMONING.

THOOOOM!

TWO MONTHS AGO.

CLOSER...

YESTERDAY.

LOOK UP, WATCHER.

IT IS INDEED A TIME OF CHANGE

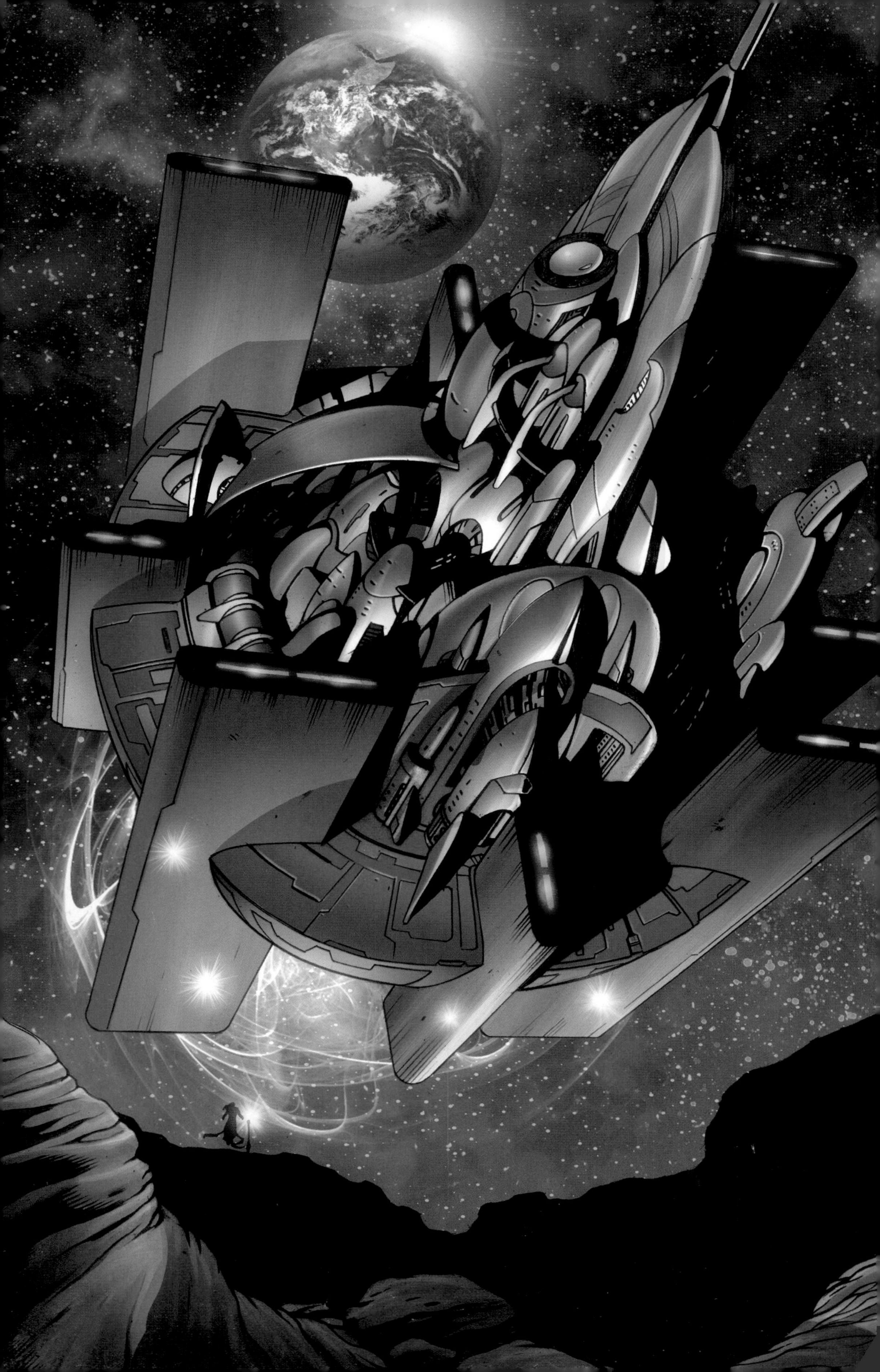

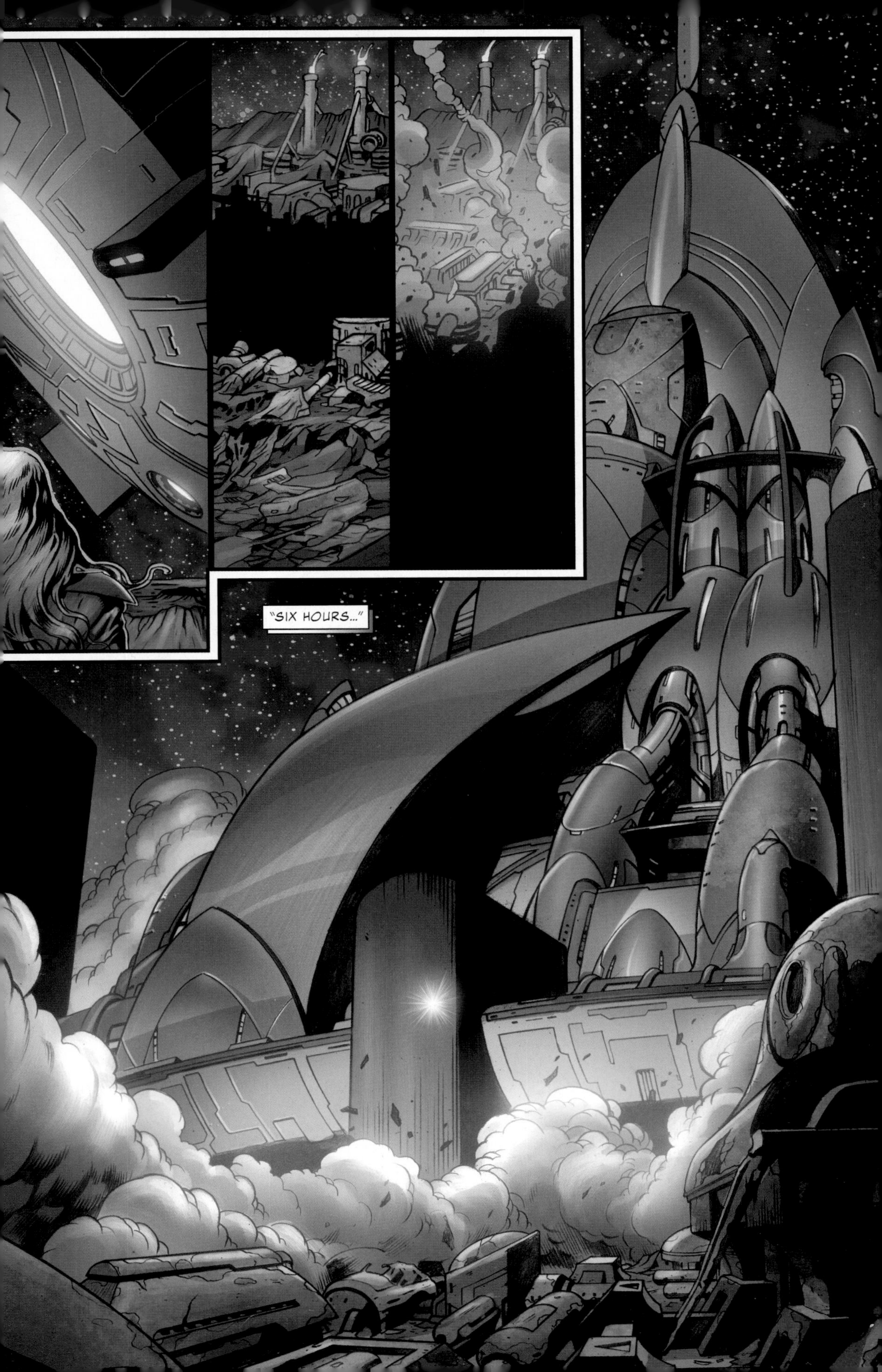
"SIX HOURS..."

THAT'S HOW LONG AGO THIS LONG-RANGE PHOTO WAS TAKEN BY A FOUNDATION SURVEILLANCE SATELLITE IN LUNAR ORBIT.

IT LANDED IN THE BLUE AREA ON THE DARK SIDE OF THE MOON...SO WE'VE GOT THIS BEFORE ANYONE ELSE.

QUESTIONS?

ANY IDEA WHAT IT IS?

BASED ON ITS PROFILE, MY FIRST GUESS WOULD BE AN EXPLORATION OR COLONIZATION VESSEL...

I SUPPOSE IT COULD BE A MINING OPERATION... HELIUM-3, MAYBE...

I HONESTLY DON'T KNOW.

OH, I KNOW WHERE THIS IS HEADED.

ONE SMALL STEP...

EXACTLY.

WHO'S UP FOR A WALK ON THE MOON?

30 MINUTES LATER.

HERE WE GO...

FIRST STAGE SEPARATION IN TWENTY-FIVE SECONDS, BEN...

HEH. JUST LIKE OLD TIMES.

LATER.
LUNAR ORBIT.

THERE IT IS.

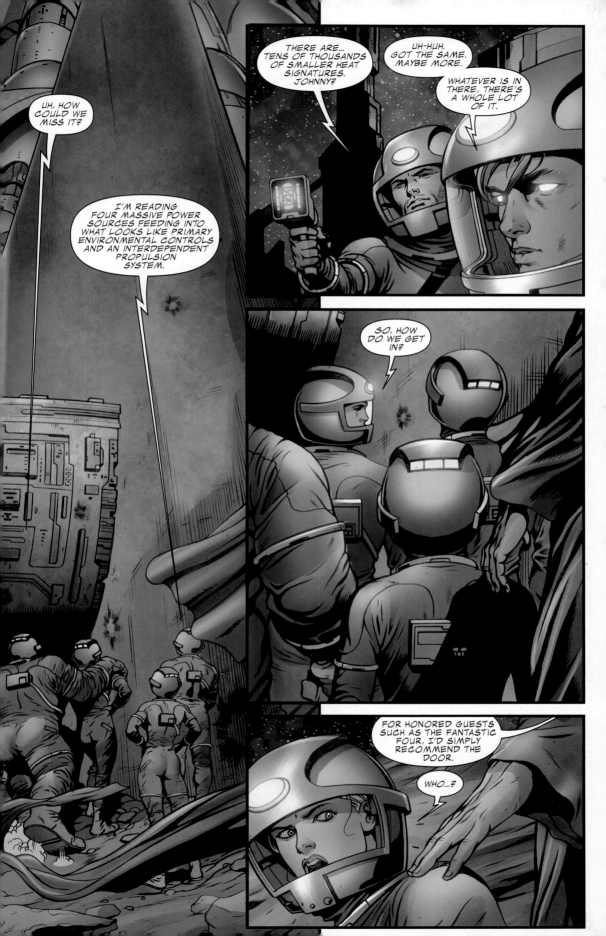

UH, HOW COULD WE MISS IT?

I'M READING FOUR MASSIVE POWER SOURCES FEEDING INTO WHAT LOOKS LIKE PRIMARY ENVIRONMENTAL CONTROLS AND AN INTERDEPENDENT PROPULSION SYSTEM.

THERE ARE... TENS OF THOUSANDS OF SMALLER HEAT SIGNATURES. JOHNNY?

UH-HUH. GOT THE SAME. MAYBE MORE.

WHATEVER IS IN THERE, THERE'S A WHOLE LOT OF IT.

SO, HOW DO WE GET IN?

FOR HONORED GUESTS SUCH AS THE FANTASTIC FOUR, I'D SIMPLY RECOMMEND THE DOOR.

WHO...?

I AM DAL DAMOC...THE WAYFINDER, LOYAL SERVANT AND PROXY FOR OUR KING, BLACK BOLT, DURING HIS ABSENCE FROM THIS SYSTEM.

I AM THE SUMMONER.

THE HERALD OF A NEW INHUMAN AGE.

WELCOME TO THE UNIVERSAL CITY.

GREAT. JUST WHAT WE NEED... ANOTHER STUPID CITY.

HEY!

WHAT YOU'RE STANDING ON, I CAN SEE IT...YOU'VE CONSTRUCTED A PERPETUAL MOTION PLANAR CONSTRUCT THAT DOESN'T REQUIRE CONSTANT THOUGHT. IT'S SO SIMPLE...

WHY HAVEN'T I EVER THOUGHT OF THAT?

I THINK THE BETTER QUESTION IS WHY WOULD A WOMAN SUCH AS YOURSELF EVER LET HER FEET TOUCH THE GROUND?

BETTER?

GREAT.

CAN WE GO INSIDE NOW?

FOLLOW ME. I'LL SHOW YOU THE WAY.

THE SIZE OF THIS VESSEL IS STAGGERING...

WHAT RACE CREATED IT?

RACES, DR. RICHARDS.... RACES.

WHEN THE FOUR BECAME ONE, A NEW MONOCULTURE OF DESTINY WAS CREATED, INDIVIDUAL ROLES WERE REDEFINED.

WHAT A PERSON USED TO BE, NO LONGER MATTERED... NOW YOU HAVE TO ASK YOURSELF, "HOW DO I BEST SERVE THE UNIVERSAL COLLECTIVE?"

HERE IS ONE ANSWER.

ONCE A POLITICIAN FOR A MINOR FACTION, HE BECAME IRRELEVANT DURING UNIFICATION.

NOW HE SERVES AS THE THRESHOLD BETWEEN THIS PLACE AND ALL OTHERS.

AMAZING.

HE IS *ELDRAC*, THE DOORWAY.

NECESSARY. THERE IS NO PLACE FOR REDUNDANCY HERE.

I TAKE IT YOU'RE AWARE OF THE ORIGINS OF THE INHUMANS?

OF COURSE.

THEN YOU KNOW, ALL OF THIS STARTED WITH THE KREE...

"...AND THEIR EXPERIMENTATION ON EARLY HUMANS--HOMO ANTECESSOR--BECAUSE OF MAN'S UNIQUE GENETIC POTENTIAL."

YES. AN OBSERVATION THE KREE MADE FROM THEIR PARALLAX-CLASS SCIENCE BASE THAT WAS LOCATED ON URANUS. I'M WELL AWARE OF...

WHAT MOST PEOPLE DO NOT KNOW--WHAT YOU DO NOT KNOW, DR. RICHARDS--IS THAT THIS KREE EXPERIMENTATION WAS NOT CARRIED OUT FROM A SINGLE BASE AND ON A SINGLE SPECIES, BUT ON MANY BASES AND ON MANY SPECIES.

SUCCESS... WAS ACHIEVED WITH *FIVE.*

FIVE?

"THE COMMON BELIEF, ONE SHARED BY ALMOST ALL KREE ELITE IN THE SACRED HALLS OF HALA, WAS THAT THE SUPREME INTELLIGENCE WAS DOING THIS TO BUILD SENTIENT WEAPONS.

"BUT THE SUPREMOR, YOU SEE... HE HAD OTHER PLANS--SECRET PLANS INVOLVING THE LONG VIEW OF THE KREE RACE."

HE WAS NOT INTERESTED IN SIMPLY PLAYING *GOD* AT THE BASE GENETIC LEVEL OF VARIOUS SPECIES. HE WAS INTERESTED IN *TRANSFORMATION.*

A RESPONSE TO A SPECIFIC CATALYST.

YOU'RE TALKING ABOUT TERRIGENESIS.

"YES. FOR US, THAT CATALYST WAS EXPOSURE TO THE MISTS OF THE TERRIGEN CRYSTALS.

"FOR OTHERS, IT WAS SOMETHING ELSE."

"ONE RACE UNDERWENT *ISOGENESIS*, CAUSED BY INJECTING THE EXTRACT OF THE ISOGEN ORBS.

"FOR ANOTHER, ONE DROP OF THE IRREPLACEABLE, DILUTED WATER FROM THE DORMANT AMPHOGEN WELL CAUSED *AMPHOGENESIS*.

"AND IN ANOTHER, *ANTIGENESIS* BROUGHT ON BY CONSUMING THE NECTAR OF THE NIGHTBLOOMS FROM THE ANTIGEN TREE.

"AND THEN THERE WAS THE ETERNAL CHANGE-- *EXOGENESIS*--THAT COMES FROM INHALING THE EXOGEN SPICE."

THE SUPREME INTELLIGENCE INTENDED FOR US TO BE SOMETHING MORE THAN JUST WEAPONS, HE INTENDED FOR US TO BE A FERTILE SOIL...

A GENETIC HARVESTING GROUND.

A WAY TO REIGNITE STAGNANT KREE EVOLUTION.

WE GOT COMPANY!

EASY, BEN.

DO YOU UNDERSTAND? TOGETHER, WITH WE EARTHBOUND *INHUMANS,* THE PEOPLE OF THIS CITY REPRESENT SALVATION FOR A DYING RACE.

OH, MY GOD...

YOU'RE BEGINNING TO SENSE THE SCOPE OF IT, AREN'T YOU?

EVEN NOW, BLACK BOLT RETURNS TO CLOSE THE CIRCLE. THE INHUMANS OF ATTILAN TRAVEL TO THE HOMEWORLD, HALA.

TO SAVE THE *KREE?*

TO CRUSH THEM UNDER HIS HEEL.

WHATEVER THE SUPREME INTELLIGENCE INTENDED, BLACK BOLT WILL LEAD US ON A NEW PATH.

WE ARE HIS PEOPLE, A TRIBE UNTO OURSELVES.

THE UNIVERSAL INHUMANS.

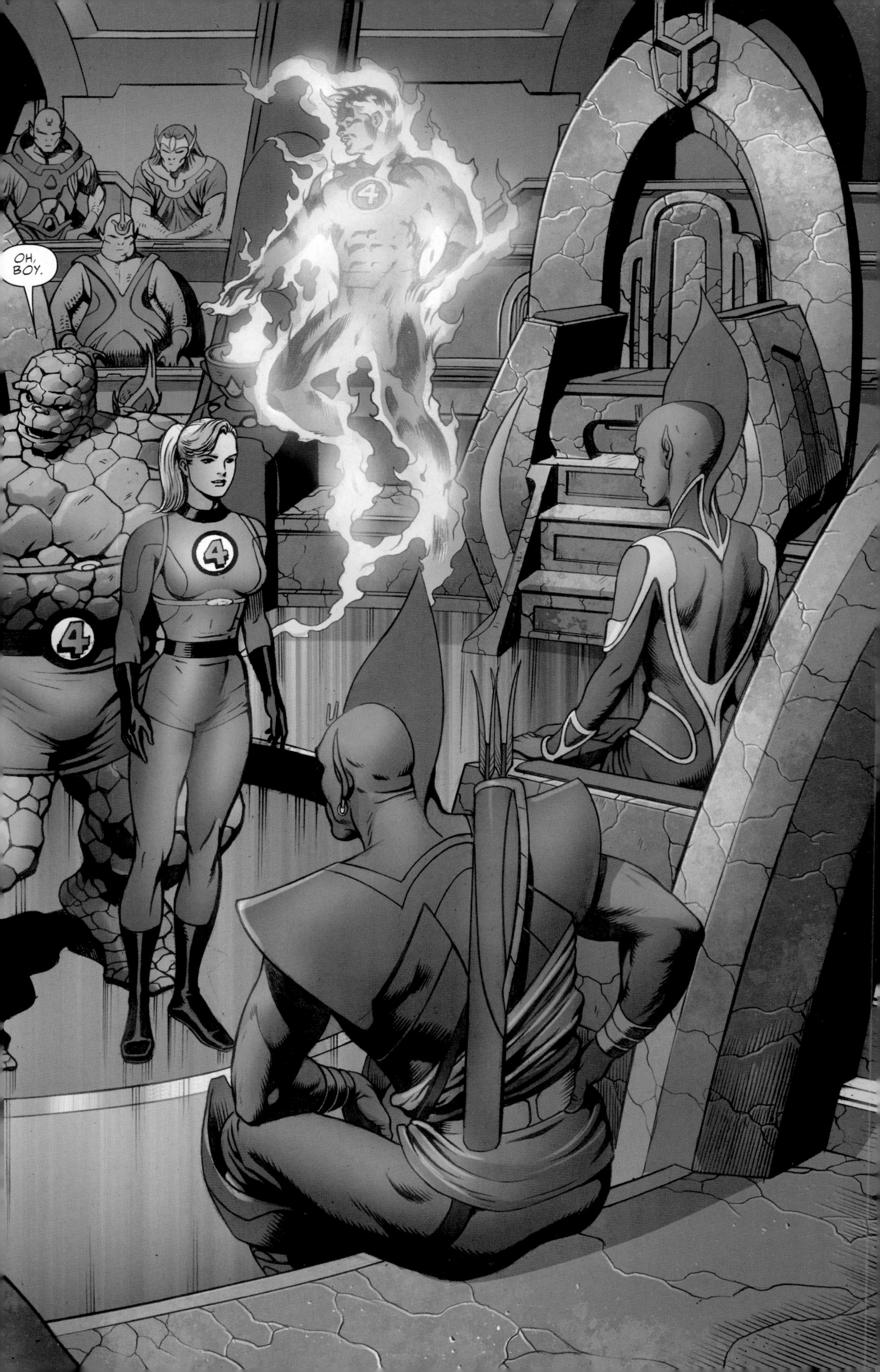
OH, BOY.

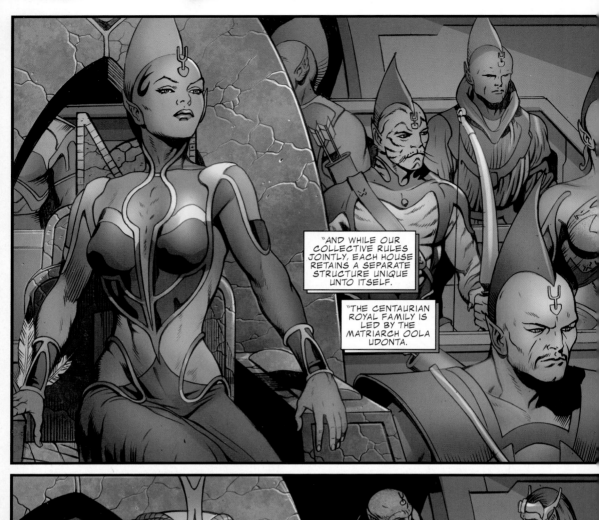

"AND WHILE OUR COLLECTIVE RULES JOINTLY, EACH HOUSE RETAINS A SEPARATE STRUCTURE UNIQUE UNTO ITSELF.

"THE CENTAURIAN ROYAL FAMILY IS LED BY THE MATRIARCH OOLA UDONTA.

"THE RULING MOORD COUNCIL IS PRESIDED OVER BY THE BADOON QUEEN, ALADI KO EKE.

"ONOMI WHITEMANE IS FIRST CHAIR OF THE KYMELLIAN WHITE ROOM.

"AND THE GODDESS AVOE RULES THE DIRE WRAITHS."

THOUGH WE ARE ALL DIFFERENT, WITHIN EACH OF US LIES A DISTINCT GENETIC MARKER... SOMETHING WE ALL SHARE.

YOU SEE, WE WERE CONSTRUCTED WITH A DORMANT MYTHOLOGY-- SHARED VISUAL IMPRINTS LEFT BY THOSE WHO MADE US.

A GROUP MEMORY?

A DESTINY, HUMAN.

FIVE QUEENS FOR THE ONE KING.

THE ONE KING WHO RETURNS FROM THE FOREVER NIGHT.

AND UNDER HIS BANNER WE WILL CLAIM OUR HOLY LAND, NEW HALA.

SO YOU SEE, DR. RICHARDS, BLACK BOLT IS RETURNING SOON...AND THEN, AS FORETOLD, WE WILL ALL BE TOGETHER FOR THE FIRST TIME.

A NEW PEOPLE IN A NEW LAND.

HERE...ON THE BLUE AREA OF THE MOON?

NO... SOMEPLACE BETTER.

OH, NO...

"NOW GO, AND SPREAD THE WORD OF HIS COMING RETURN."

- THERE ARE ROUGHLY ONE HUNDRED AND TEN THOUSAND CITIZENS LIVING ON THE INHUMAN CITY-SHIP. POPULATION ESTIMATES ARE:

  - 22,000 CENTAURIANS (11,500 MALE, 10,500 FEMALE)
  - 17,250 BADOON (9,250 MALE, 8,000 FEMALE)
  - 26,250 KYMELLIANS (13,000 MALE, 13,250 FEMALE)
  - 44,500 DIRE WRAITHS (31,250 MALE, 13,250 FEMALE)

- THERE ARE CURRENTLY 726 INHUMAN PRISONERS LOCATED ON THE BLACK LEVEL OF THE CITY-SHIP.

- THE LIGHT BRIGADE IS AN ELITE GROUP COMPRISED OF THE SIX GREATEST INHUMAN WARRIORS. EACH LIGHT BRIGADE IS FORMED TO TAKE PART IN A RITUAL CALLED THE OFFERING.

  THE OFFERING TAKES PLACE ONCE EVERY GENERATION. DURING THE CEREMONY, THE LIGHT BRIGADE TAKES ON AN ENDLESS SUCCESSION OF TRIALS IN ORDER TO INTERNALLY PROVE THE WORTHINESS OF THE INHUMAN COLLECTIVE. THE OFFERING ENDS WITH THE DEATH OF THE LAST LIVING MEMBER OF THE LIGHT BRIGADE.

  NO LIGHT BRIGADE HAS EVER SURVIVED LONGER THAN A YEAR.

homepad

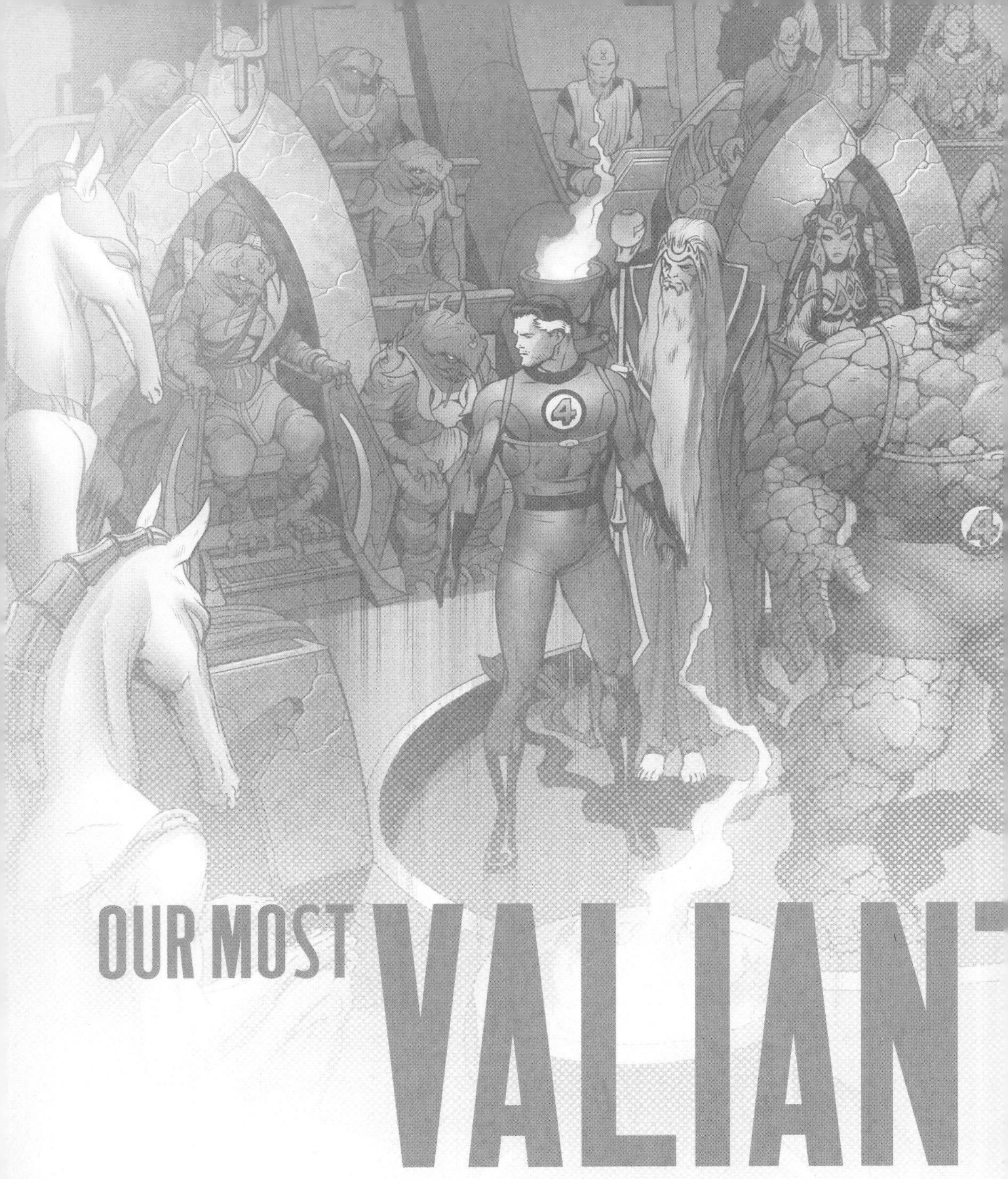

OUR MOST VALIANT

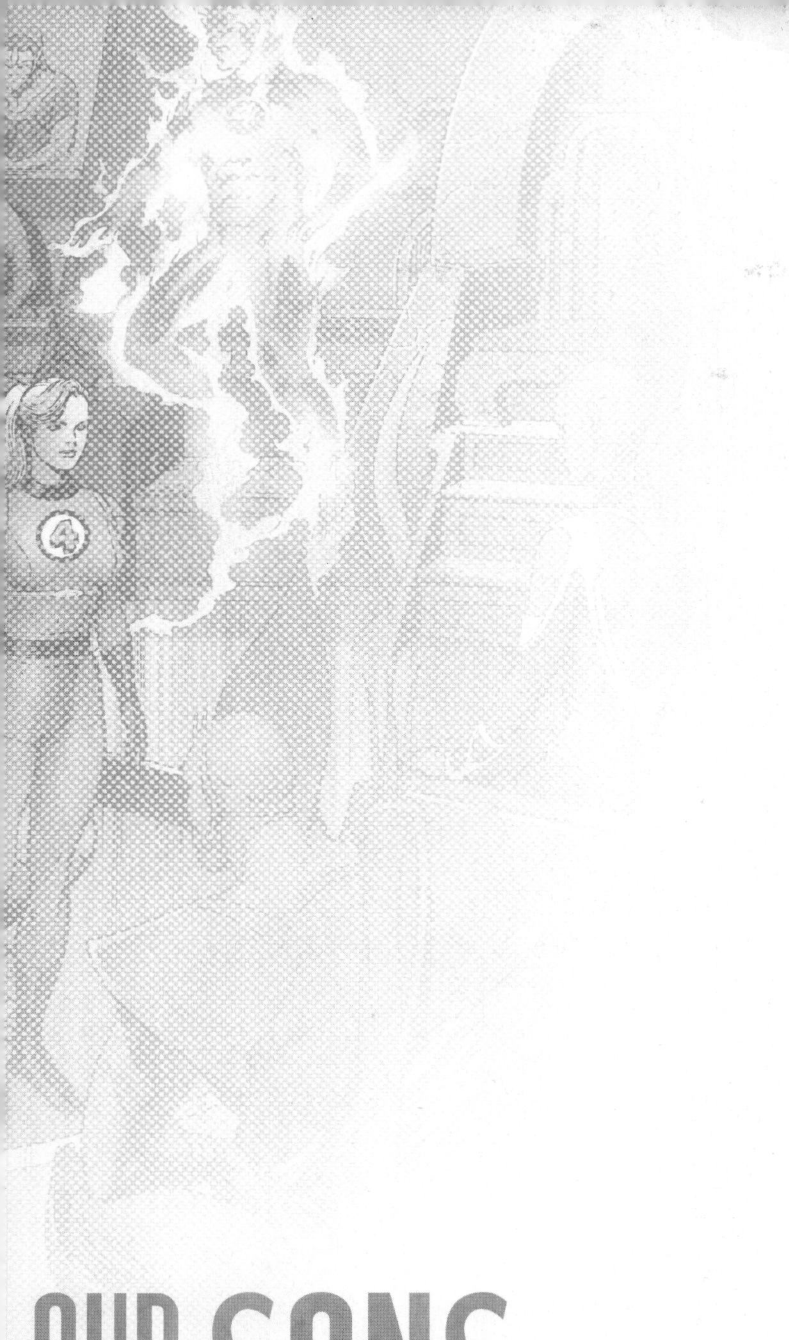

OUR SONS AND DAUGHTERS

"EXACTLY WHY AM I TELLING YOU THIS AGAIN?"

"I DID ASK NICELY."

"FINE. EVERYTHING SEEMED COMPLETELY NORMAL.

"NOTHING OUT OF THE ORDINARY AT ALL.

EXIT

SO... MAYBE WE COULD GO BACK TO YOUR PLACE?

SURE. I'LL DRIVE.

"AND THIS WAS WHERE?"

"A NEW PLACE...

"SOME STATE-OF-THE-ART CHAIN CLUB.

BEHOLD! THE WORDS OF THE ANTI-PRIEST:

EQUILIBRIUM AND THERMODYNAMICS HAVE LEFT YOU WITH NO OTHER CHOICE...

"IT WAS AN ALL-INCLUSIVE PERFORMANCE ART/SPA/SELF-HELP SHRINE/BAR CALLED THE OTHER SIDE OF ZERO.

DO YOU WANT TO BE A SLAVE TO FATE...A SERVANT TO YOUR EVENTUAL DEMISE?

OR DO YOU WANT NEW RULES FOR A NEW LIFE?

"THE SCENE WAS WEIRD AND DEAD, SO WE CAME HERE..."

BOOP!

WANT A DRINK?

NO.

SUIT YOURSELF...

SO, WHAT DO YOU THINK OF THE BAXTER BUILDING?

VERY COOL.

I LOVE GADGETS.

THEN YOU'RE DEFINITELY IN THE RIGHT PLACE.

AND YOU'RE NOT GOING TO BELIEVE THE VIEW FROM MY ROOM...

AH.

THERE YOU ARE.

I CAN FEEL THE CONNECTION... MAKING SOMETHING MOVE IN ME.

NATASHA?

HEY!

GET AWAY FROM THERE!

THAT'S THE NEGATIVE ZONE PORTAL! YOU HAVE NO IDEA HOW DANGEROUS THAT THING IS!

OF COURSE I DO...IT'S WHY I'M HERE.

WHAT?

CRAKKT!

THEY KNEW YOU'D BE AT THE CLUB THIS EVENING... AND BECAUSE OF THAT, AND BECAUSE I'M BEAUTIFUL, THEY CHOSE ME.

WE'RE PREDICTABLE BECAUSE WE'RE SO SIMPLE, JOHNNY.

YOU JUST WANT TO ENJOY LIFE...

AND I JUST WANT TO DIE.

HHMMMM MMM

SEE, THERE'S A NATURAL ORDER OF THINGS.

FROM A DENSE, HOT STATE OUR REALITY EXPLODED INTO EXISTENCE. BUT AS SOON AS IT WAS BORN, OUR UNIVERSE BEGAN DYING.

AND THE SLOW, AGONIZING EXTINCTION SPIRAL CALLED EXPANSION WILL END IN THE HEAT DEATH OF EVERYTHING.

BUT THROUGH THIS GATE, THE NATURAL ORDER IS REVERSED.

HERE, YOU DIE. IN THE NEGATIVE ZONE, YOU CAN LIVE.

THE ANTI-PRIEST TAUGHT ME THIS AND I BELIEVE HIM.

HE PUT A WORD IN ME. A SECRET WORD...

THIS IS A NEW AGE.

DO YOU WANT TO HEAR...?

HEAR...

HEAR...

IT...

OH, #%$@

AH

NIGH

HU

LUUUH

SSSSS

URK!

BLOORP

OKAY...

JOHNNY GOES TO BAR. JOHNNY GETS GIRL. GIRL TURNS OUT TO BE A BUG MONSTER. BUG MONSTER DISAPPEARS THROUGH THE HOLE. JOHNNY NEVER KISSED THE BUG.

I'M GOING TO CALL THAT A WIN.

BLOOP.

NO. DON'T SHUT DOWN THE PORTAL...

I'M GOING IN AFTER THEM.

BORP!

YEAH? AND DID YOU SEE THAT DEVICE ONE OF THEM WAS HOLDING?

WHAT DID IT LOOK LIKE TO YOU?

BOOOP.

IT MOST DEFINITELY WAS A BOMB.

JUST HOLD THE GATE OPEN FOR FIVE MINUTES. OKAY?

MY MESS... I'M GONNA FIX IT.

BLOP.

RELAX. I'M GOING TO MAKE FLAMEBAIT OF FIVE BUGS AND I'LL BE RIGHT BACK.

NO PROBLEM.

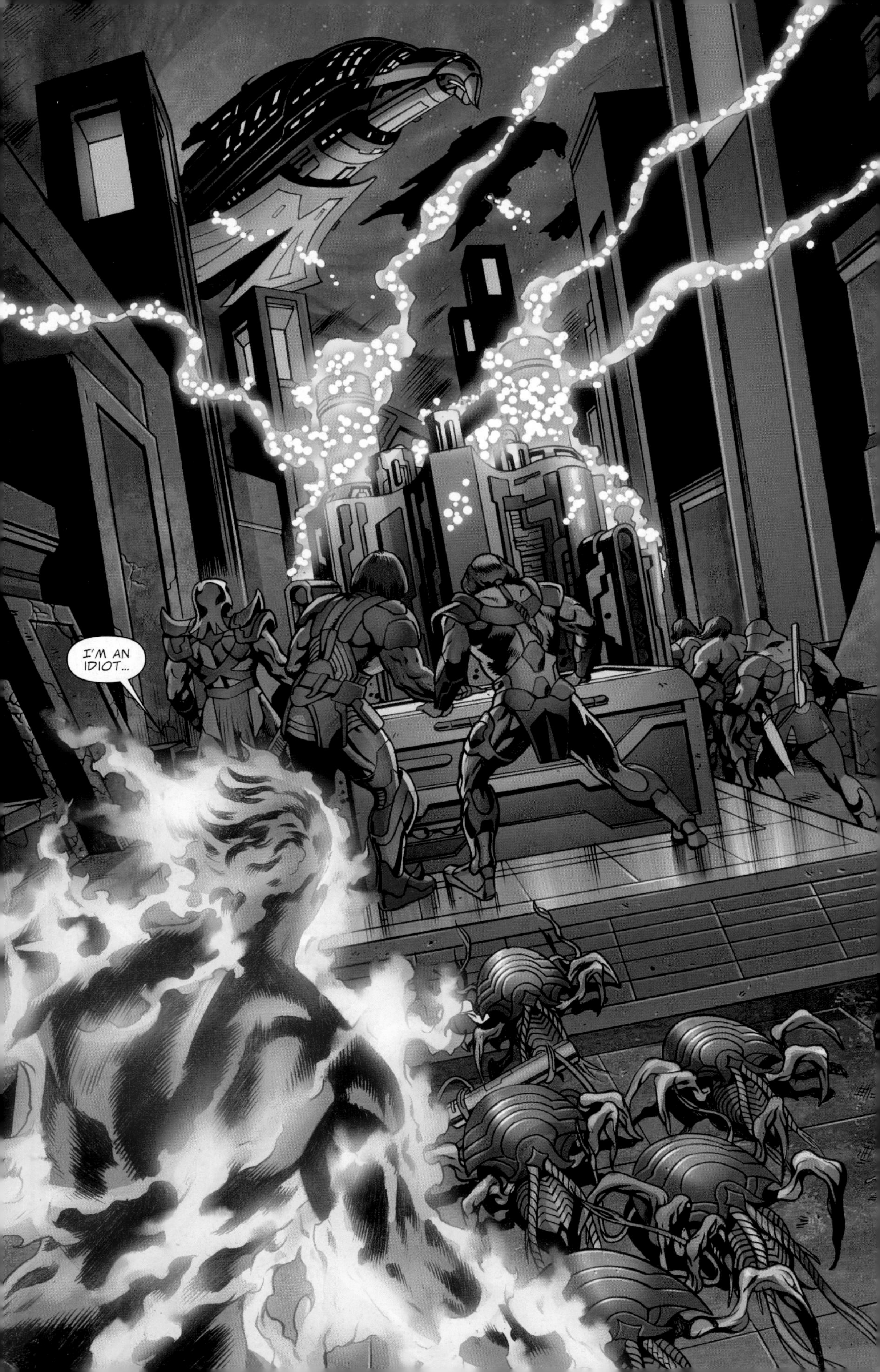
I'M AN IDIOT...

GENERAL-- THE ARMADA OF ANNIHILUS.

HEY! LOOK OUT! STOP THEM!

THEY'VE GOT A BOMB!

BAH!

LET THE HIVE SWARM...THE COSMIC CONTROL ROD POWERS OUR DEFENSES, AND THERE IS NO WAY THROUGH OUR SHIELDS.

UFFF!

WHAT...

NOOO!

BA-BBBOOOOOON!!!

UUUHH.

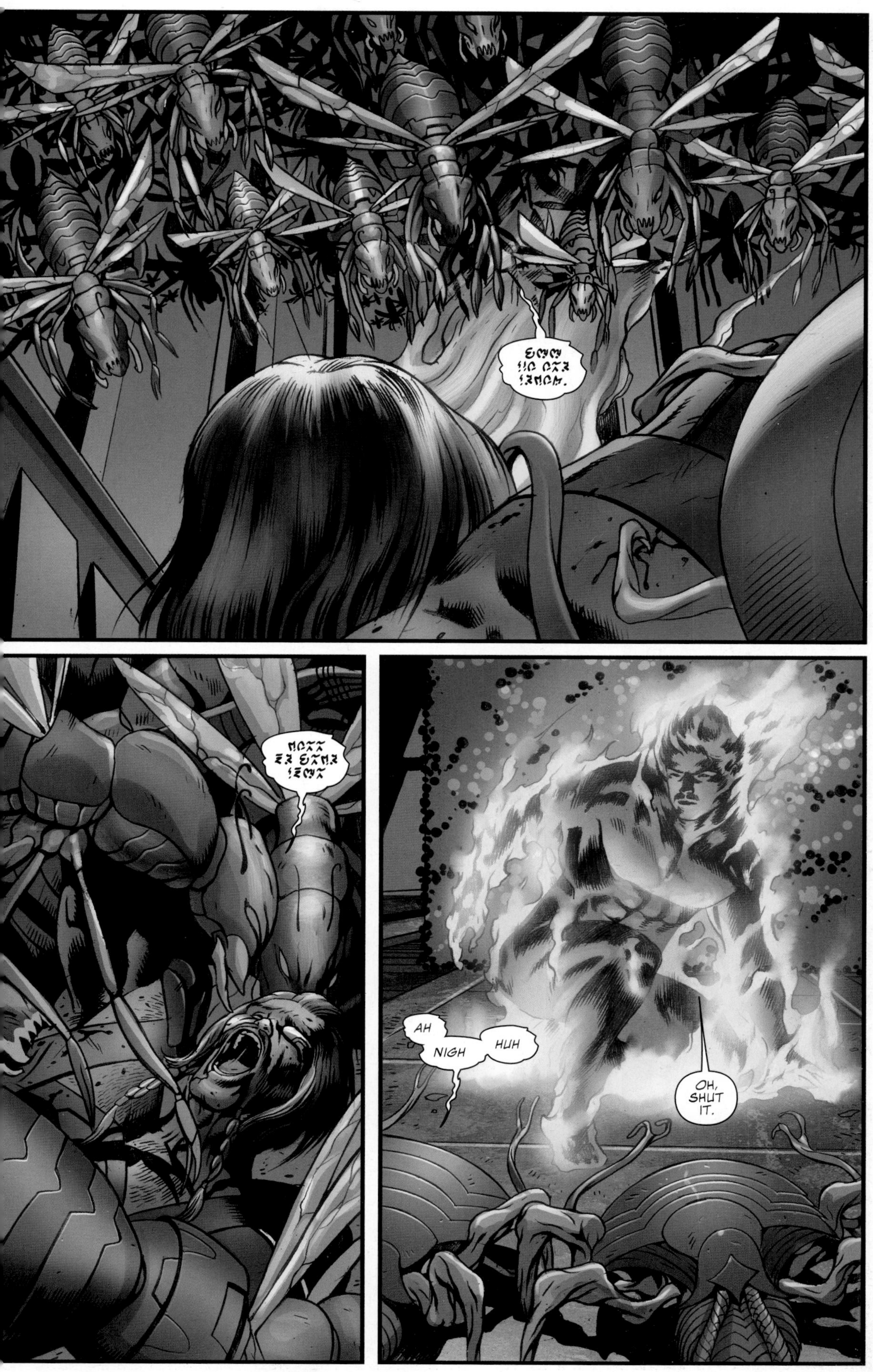
AH
NIGH
HUH
OH, SHUT IT.

SQQUEEEEE!!

SQQUEEEEE!!

SQQUEEEEE!!

UH-OH.

- THE OTHER SIDE OF ZERO IS THE RECRUITMENT ARM FOR AN ORGANIZATION CALLED THE CULT OF THE NEGATIVE ZONE.

- THE MARK III NEGATIVE ZONE PORTAL POSSESSES THE FOLLOWING FEATURES AND IMPROVEMENTS: A FASTER BOOT CYCLE, EMERGENCY TRANSPARENT VIBRANIUM SHIELDING, AND A DECOMPRESSION BUFFER.

- THE ANNIHILATION WAVE ARMADA HAS BEEN REBUILT TO PRE-CRUNCH ASSAULT LEVELS.

- A STATE OF WAR EXISTS BETWEEN THE FORCES OF THE REBORN ANNIHILUS AND BLASTAAR, SELF-DESCRIBED KING OF THE NEGATIVE ZONE.

- THE LEVEL 42 NEGATIVE ZONE PRISON STATION HAS BEEN EXPANDED INTO A...

WAIT A SECOND...

homepad

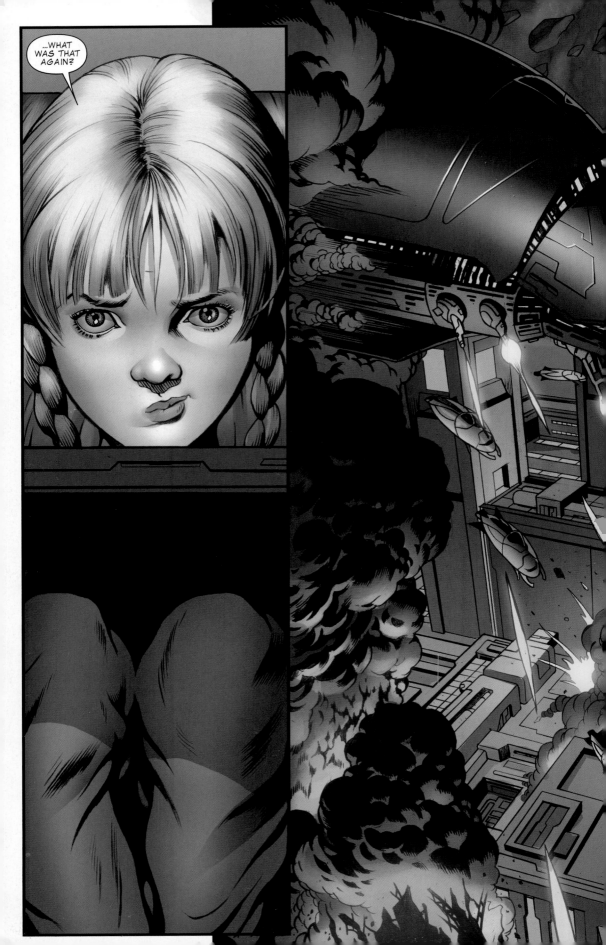

...WHAT WAS THAT AGAIN?

I SAID, THEY'VE EXPANDED THE NEGATIVE ZONE PRISON INTO A CITY.

AND THAT MAKES FOUR.

I GUESS THAT'S SETTLED.

WHAT?

NOTHING. WHAT HAPPENED THEN?

WELL, CONSIDERING I DIDN'T STOP THE BUGS FROM SETTING OFF THE BOMB, THE ANNIHILATION WAVE WAS POURING INTO THE BASE, AND MY FIVE MINUTES WAS ALMOST UP...

I ACCEPTED THAT IT WAS NOT MY DAY AND GOT THE HECK OUT OF DODGE.

"ANY PROBLEMS THERE?"

"NOT REALLY."

CLOSE IT!

CLOSE IT NOW!

WHY ARE YOU SO INTERESTED IN ALL THIS, VAL?

YOU KNOW ME, UNCLE JOHNNY... GOTTA KEEP LEARNING. GOTTA FEED THE BEAST.

UH-HUH.

YOU SURE THERE ISN'T SOMETHING WE SHOULD BE CONCERNED ABOUT?

HOW WOULD I KNOW SOMETHING LIKE THAT?

AND SOUTH OF THE BAXTER BUILDING, THE HERALD OF MAN ESCORTS AN ENVOY TO THE PEAK.

ANDROMEDA ATTUMASEN-- ANDROMEDA THE SWORD-- COMES WITH A MESSAGE FROM NAMOR.

WHO ARE YOU TO CALL YOURSELF KINGS?

YOU DARE...

RUMBLE

"WHO CALLS HIMSELF KING THAT HAS NEVER FELT THE SUN ON HIS FACE?

"...THAT COWERS UNDER THE ICE AT THE BOTTOM OF THE WORLD?

"...THAT SLEEPS THROUGH THE AGE OF MAN?

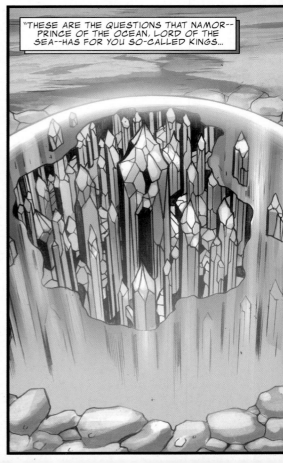
"THESE ARE THE QUESTIONS THAT NAMOR-- PRINCE OF THE OCEAN, LORD OF THE SEA--HAS FOR YOU SO-CALLED KINGS...

"WHEN YOU HAVE ANSWERS FOR HIM-- WHEN YOU COME OUT OF HIDING--HE WILL MEET YOU THEN."

LATER. THE BAXTER BUILDING.

GOT A MINUTE?

REED, YEAH, SURE.

WELL?

...

I DON'T KNOW WHAT I WAS THINKING.

YOU SHOULD HAVE COME TO GET ME OR BEN...

WE DON'T DO THESE THINGS ALONE... AND WE DON'T DO THEM IN A WAY THAT ENDANGERS OTHERS.

I KNOW, IT'S JUST THAT IT WAS MY FAULT IT HAPPENED. I WAS ANGRY AND WANTED TO...

...

OH, MAN, I CAN'T BELIEVE...I LEFT THE PORTAL OPEN...

AND ALL THE KIDS WERE IN THE BUILDING...

GOD, I REALLY AM SORRY, REED.

HEY, I LOVE THAT YOU DIVE IN HEAD FIRST, JOHNNY...WE ALL DO.

BUT YOU HAVE TO START PAYING ATTENTION TO WHAT'S GOING ON.

WHAT DO YOU MEAN?

EVERYTHING IS CHANGING, JOHNNY. *EVERYTHING* AND *EVERYONE.*

BEN, SUE...THE KIDS.

I'M NOT SURE IF I EVEN HAVE THE WORDS TO EXPLAIN WHAT I'M GOING THROUGH...

AND AS EVERYTHING CHANGES AROUND YOU, IT'S INEVITABLE THAT YOU'LL EXPERIENCE SOMETHING LIKE THIS AS WELL.

AND WHAT AM I SUPPOSED TO DO WHEN THAT HAPPENS, REED?

IT'S SIMPLE, JOHNNY.

YOU ASK YOURSELF A QUESTION...

"WHAT IS IT YOU *STAND* FOR?

"WHEN YOU CAN ANSWER THAT, THEN YOU'LL KNOW."

AND IN THE BLUE AREA OF THE MOON, A RITUAL OF IMMOLATION:

THE OFFERING.

FIVE BRIDES AND ONE KING, LET THE NUMBER BE SIX.

SIX WARRIORS FOR SACRIFICE.

THE LIGHT BRIGADE.

"HOW CAN WE CLAIM A WORLD IF WE ARE NOT WORTHY?

"AND HOW CAN WE BE WORTHY IF WE HAVEN'T ATTEMPTED THE IMPOSSIBLE?"

ELDRAC... GIVE US A BATTLE THAT WE CANNOT WIN.

"THE BLOOD-PRICE WILL BE PAID... THE VERY BEST WE HAVE TO OFFER:

"OUR MOST VALIANT.

"OUR SONS AND DAUGHTERS."

AND SO, IN THE NEGATIVE ZONE, THE WAR OF FOUR CITIES BEGINS.

COVER GALLERY

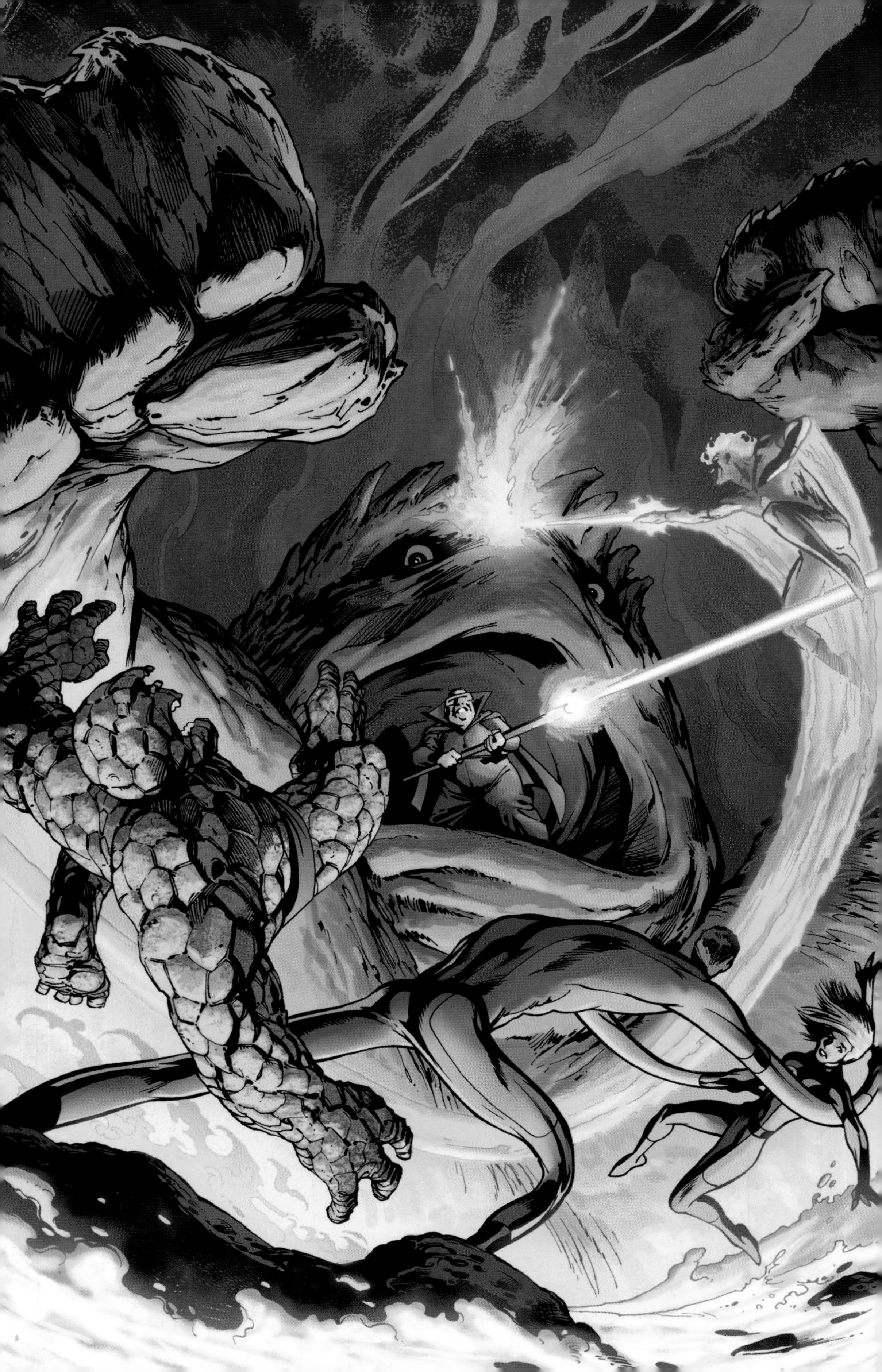

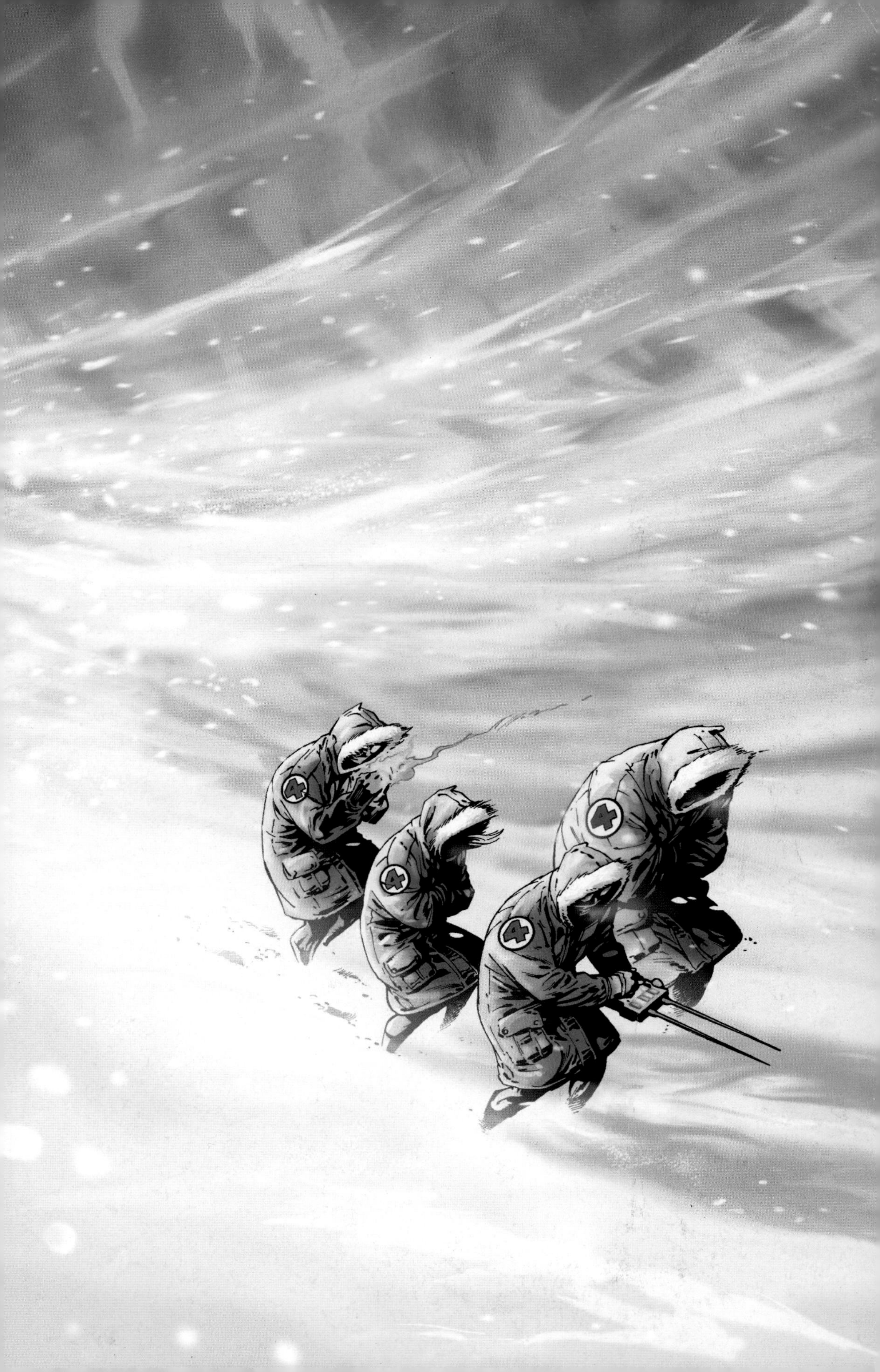

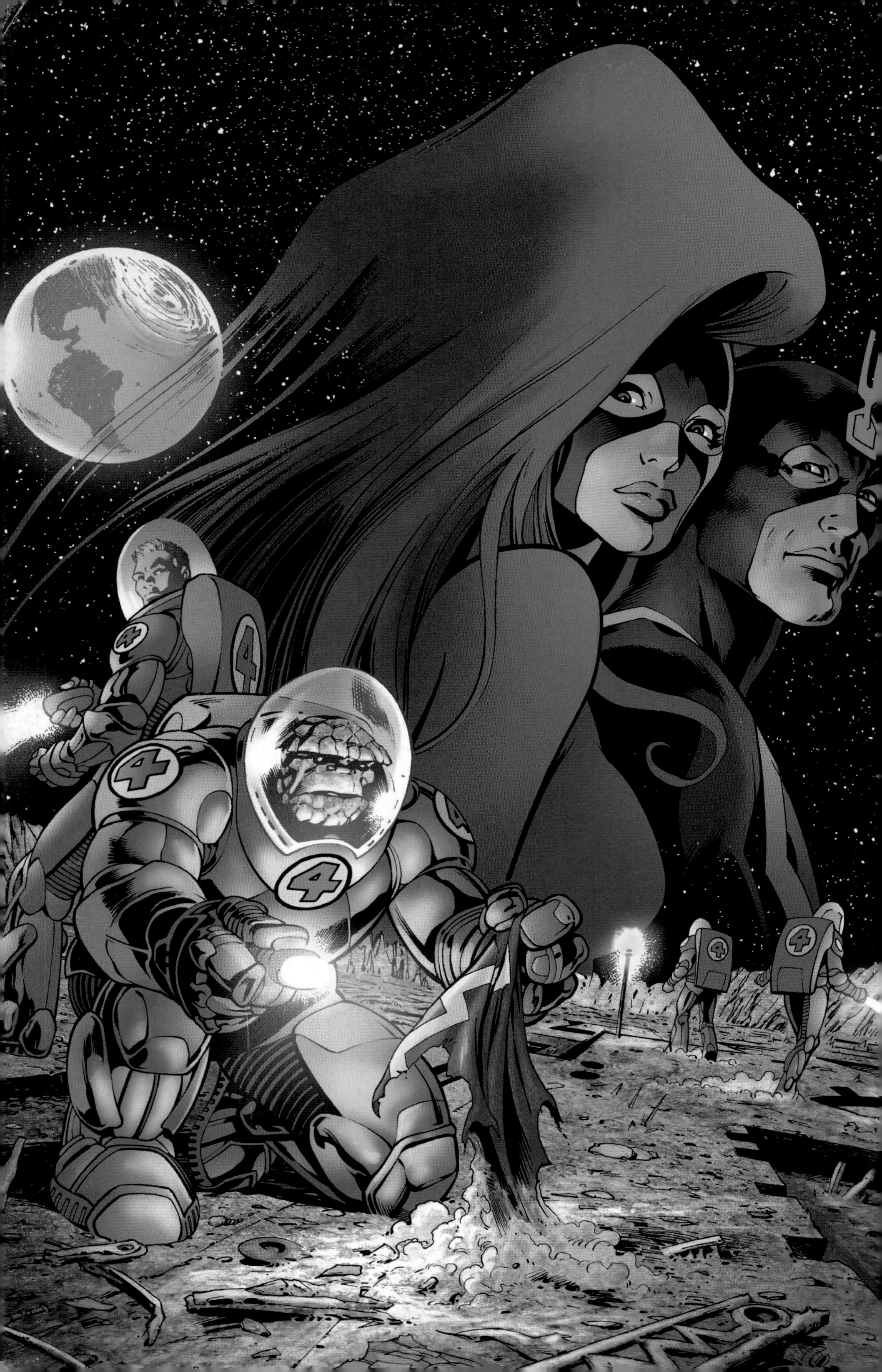

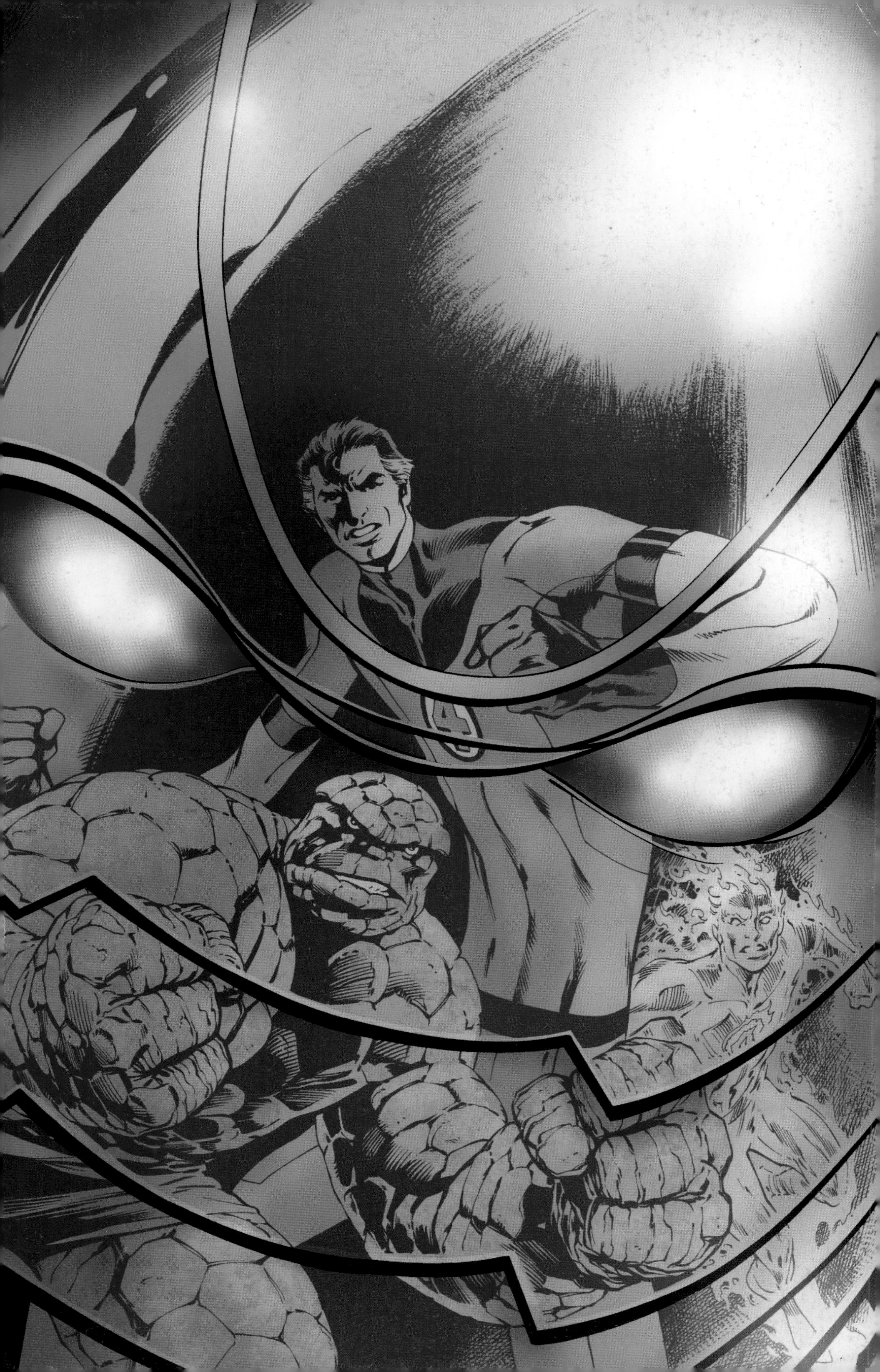

#575 WOMEN OF MARVEL: CELEBRATING SEVEN DECADES VARIANT: JELENA KEVIC DJURDJEVIC